ORDER IN THE COURT

HISTORY AND SOCIETY IN *LA PRINCESSE DE CLÈVES*

STANFORD FRENCH AND ITALIAN STUDIES

editor

ALPHONSE JUILLAND

editorial board

BEVERLY ALLEN
MARC BERTRAND
BRIGITTE CAZELLES
ROBERT GREER COHN
JEAN-PIERRE DUPUY
JOHN FRECCERO
RENÉ GIRARD
ROBERT HARRISON
RALPH HESTER
PAULINE NEWMAN-GORDON
PIERRE SAINT-AMAND
JEFFREY SCHNAPP
MICHEL SERRES
CAROLYN SPRINGER

managing editor

KATARINA KIVEL

volume XLVII

DEPARTMENT OF FRENCH AND ITALIAN
STANFORD UNIVERSITY

ORDER IN THE COURT

HISTORY AND SOCIETY IN *LA PRINCESSE DE CLÈVES*

LAURENCE A. GREGORIO

1986
ANMA LIBRI

PQ
1805
.L5
A755
1986

Stanford French and Italian Studies is a collection of scholarly publications devoted to the study of French and Italian literature and language, culture and civilization. Occasionally it will allow itself excursions into related Romance areas.

Stanford French and Italian Studies will publish books, monographs, and collections of articles centering around a common theme, and is also open to scholars associated with academic institutions other than Stanford.

The collection is published for the Department of French and Italian, Stanford University by Anma Libri.

© 1986 by ANMA Libri & Co.
P.O. Box 876, Saratoga, Calif. 95071
All rights reserved.
LC 86-71858
ISBN 0-915838-63-X
Printed in the United States of America

Acknowledgements

First and foremost, I wish to express my gratitude to Professor Jean V. Alter of the University of Pennsylvania for his great generosity and his tireless concern for my work. His kind friendship and unsparing criticism gave cohesion to a mere collection of ideas. I also thank my friends and colleagues at Gettysburg College for their support and encouragement, and I thank the administration of the College for its material aid in the publication of this work. To Bill Wilson, Dick Wood and Kim Breighner, I express great appreciation for their technical help and computer wizardry. Finally, I thank everyone in my family for the moral support I relied upon during drafting and revision.

*To my wife, Marcia,
and our children, Joseph, Julie and Elena*

Preface

In a sense, all narration is the writing of history, or at the very least, it reflects something of the process of writing history. When a novelist sets pen to paper giving words to a storyteller or narrator, the resulting fiction incorporates the make-believe notion that whatever is told has happened at some point, and can be believed, if only within the boundaries of the text's world. The question of whether the events recounted in a literary text did, in fact, occur in the world outside the text is not of immediate concern to the critic of fiction. To phrase it another way, the veracity of the novel is of much less importance to the student of literature than other things. One of those things is the organization or presentation of the text: not so much its historical content as its historical vision or technique. This particular facet of narratology becomes all the more interesting and complex in the study of a work which is counted among those known as "historical novels," one which uses history to create and enhance the illusion that causes fiction to pass for history or to stand beside it in a narrative continuum.

The purpose of this study is to shed light upon the dynamics of historiography in such a novel, *La Princesse de Clèves* by Mme de Lafayette. Along the way, other germane topics will necessarily present themselves for discussion. Most notable is the social context which the novel sets for the unfolding of action: without it the text would be a love story lacking parameters to define it, a psychological study of the individual, bereft of the interplay of many of its forces. As it is portrayed, society is the dynamic setting which gives life to oppositions in the text and becomes a part of history.

The edition of *La Princesse de Clèves* upon which this work is based is the one established and annotated by Antoine Adam in the Bibliothèque de la Pléiade collection entitled *Romanciers du XVIIe siècle* (Paris: Gallimard, 1958). All references to the novel will be to this edition and will be noted parenthetically in the course of this study. The principal reason for this choice is not that the text's written language is that of the seventeenth century (though this does offer advantages), but that this edition includes the prefatory "Le Libraire au lecteur" which comments on the novel's writing and narration.[1]

The plan of the present work is easily understood. Each of the following chapters deals with an element of the novel's composition as it contributes to the chronicle of a courtly society. Hence the title chosen for this book. The first chapter addresses the topic of the novel's complex narrative strategy; the second examines the text's historiographic vision and process; third is the consideration of the novelistic world that serves as the setting for action and the pretext for narration; finally, the fourth and fifth chapters discuss action and characterization respectively.

If lengthy discourse about the topic of love in *La Princesse* is conspicuous by its absence, the reader may be assured that the omission is intentional. This is not out of disdain for the matter or unawareness of its import; rather it is because criticism has tended to investigate love in the novel to the exclusion of other significant issues, and has, in my opinion, studied it thoroughly enough. Other avenues of inquiry are open in this, the best known French novel of the seventeenth century.

---

[1] The preface, appearing inside the novel's title page, and entitled "Le Libraire au lecteur," reads as follows: "Quelque approbation qu'ait eu cette Histoire dans les lectures qu'on en a faites, l'Autheur n'a pu se résoudre à se déclarer; il a craint que son nom ne diminuast le succès de son livre. Il sçait par expérience que l'on condamne quelquefois les Ouvrages sur la médiocre opinion qu'on a de l'Autheur et il sçait aussi que la réputation de l'Autheur donne souvent du prix aux Ouvrages. Il demeure donc dans l'obscurité où il est pour laisser les jugemens plus libres et plus équitables, et il se montrera néanmoins si cette Histoire est aussi agréable au public que je l'espère" (p. 1106).

Table of Contents

1. Narration   1
2. The Gaze of History   26
3. Society: Sight and Sound   47
4. Catalysts of Action: Social Dynamics 69
5. Characterization and Absence   93
   Conclusion   111
   Bibliography   117

1. Narration

I

The narrator of *La Princesse de Clèves* is a curious and rather elusive figure. Of course we know the novelist to be a woman, but apart from the detailed portrayal of the heroine's psychological processes, which one might interpret as the expression of a woman's perspective, there are no signs to indicate that the narrator is indeed also a woman. For that matter, however, there are no explicit signs showing the storyteller to be a man, unless one were to consider as such the admiration and distance with which the heroine is ostensibly depicted. Overt signs of the narrator (references in the first person) are two in number: the first is the only mention of a singular speaking first person ("ceux que je vais nommer..." p. 1108); the other is in the plural ("...l'espérance de nos conquestes,..." p. 1111) and is seemingly intended to establish bonds with the French heritage and reading public. For the sake of clarity, we will adopt the practice of referring to the narrator in the masculine, but with the understanding that no direct signs in the narrative compel this choice. In any event, it will give the added convenience of graphically abstracting the narrator from this novel's author.

In view of the lack of information as to the gender, name or personal situation of this fictive construct, the narrator's implicit or more covert signs are all the more revealing. We know the storyteller to be intimately familiar with the past history of the French court, and passionately interested in the social goings-on of that court. He demonstrates marked concern for such matters as human psychology and ethics, with a distinct tendency to generalize in these areas by means of maxims set within the narrative.[1] Cultural affinities are maintained with the seventeenth-century French reading public in the form of assumptions made about the understanding of social priorities, cultural history, geographical and genealogical data, etc. The narrative voice does not hesitate to add detail or to correct, for the reader, misconceptions of his characters, thus showing care for the orderliness of the narrative. At the same time, he is attempting to shape the reader's interpretive process.

All of these signs contribute to clarifying the narrative pact: they offer the reader important information about the source of a story whose historicism and psychology have sparked much discussion through the ages. Nevertheless, the accumulation of these signs falls short of providing a clear temporal situation for the narrator. On the one hand, he speaks as a detached and omniscient third person, but one who must have witnessed the subtleties of facial expressions or heard the ironic remarks with which the story is replete. He speaks confidently for the characters' thoughts and emotions which are the basic matter of the novel. This feature of the narrative presupposes a more or less contemporaneous narratorial perspective.

On the other hand, the same narrator adopts a clearly historical point of view over the action, setting about a century's distance between the events and the recounting of those events.[2] This distance is lengthened explicitly by comments which discount the narrator as a firsthand witness to the events that he is relating, comments such as "...et l'on doit croire que c'étoit une beauté parfaite..." (p. 1113, in reference to the heroine upon her introduction). But the issue goes further: at many points, sometimes very crucial ones, the narrator equivocates with the faculty of omniscience which elsewhere governs the telling of the tale. Habitual and presumably authoritative reporting of characters' innermost feelings and motives is undermined by a strikingly different narrative stance—one which sounds a dissonant chord of "peut-être." And, as the narrator would have it, the shift often occurs at junctures in the action where the reader (accustomed elsewhere to total disclosure of detail) would appreciate an accurate knowledge of the motives in question:

[1] For an interesting and thorough treatment of this topic, see Jeanne Goldin, "Maximes et fonctionnement narratif dans la *Princesse de Clèves*," Papers on French Seventeenth Century Literature, 10, No. 2 (1978), 155-76.
[2] Cf. Ann M. Moore, "Temporal Structure and Reader Response in *La Princesse de Clèves*," French Review, 56, No. 4 (March 1983), 563-71.

M. de Nemours estoit de ce nombre et c'estoit peut-estre ce qui avoit donné envie à Mme de Clèves d'avoir ces tableaux. (p. 1224)

Peut-estre souhaitoit-elle, autant qu'elle le craignoit, d'y trouver M. de Nemours;... (p. 1228)

These points have a direct effect on the reader's attempt to situate the narrator chronologically. Does the narrator offer precise documentation in his capacity as a witness to the action? Or does he speak in retrospect of an era long since past? Neither question can receive a definitive answer because of the reoccurrence of subtly conflicting signs to cloud the issue.

Indeed, despite its thematic continuity and the customary air of classical homogeneity, the narrator's speech is by no means a uniform discourse. It is divided within itself, along lines which have no evident relationship with internal oppositions which we will discuss later; the division to which we now refer pertains to the different modes of discourse practiced by the narrator. The labels by which we designate these different modes may be subject to debate; however, their qualitative and chronological distinctions seem to be self-evident.

— The *historian*: in this role (or mode), the narrator is primarily the scene-setter, objectively detailing background and past events (true or fictive, intermixed) in a detached sort of retrospect; his discourse situates itself as *posterior* in time to the related story.

— The *memorialist*: this is the mode of discourse in which the story itself is recounted; it includes a third-person narration with a fixed point of view, and a more neutral type of third-person omniscient reportage, both of which relate characters' emotions, misinterpretations, etc.; this mode situates the narrator as *contemporaneous* with the action.

— The *psychologist/moralist*: this side of the narrator shows the tendency to generalize about human nature, and to deal with such issues as motivation and ethics; with its penchant for maxims and generalizations, this mode of narrative discourse is *atemporal*, unbound by the story's time scheme.

Throughout the novel, the outward guise of unity is maintained. Yet it is clear, once the heroine's story has begun, that the nature of narrative voice shows all three modes of discourse — each of which stands in opposition to the others. The contrast is most noticeable as regards the chronological setting of narration. As we shall see, this multiplicity of narratorial roles is our first indicator of an implicit definition of the nature of the text; indeed, a narrator, rendered timeless and posing alternately as historian, memorialist, or psychologist, produces a literary work which can comfortably accommodate all these modes, i.e. a novel.

Thus, from an extrinsic point of view, a narrator without precise temporal setting is quite suitable for abstracting fiction from fact in a historical novel—after all, the heroine's story is something of a non-real (or fictive) fairy-tale situated against a genuine historical background; the narrative voice is as removed from time, and therefore just as fictional, as the love story being told. Given the novel's implicit juxtaposition of historicity and fiction, the temporal "non-reality" of the narrator would seem best suited to the text's overall purposes.

This consideration, however, gives little help, if any, to the reader who seeks a consistent understanding of the novel's narrative plan. The fact remains that, up to this point, we have seen a narrator with no clear identity of gender or time, and with no consistent justification of knowledge (e.g. omniscience, eyewitness testimony, etc.). To dwell within the bounds of the text itself, and extrinsic interpretations aside, a concise and comprehensive assessment of the narrative strategy is a task made difficult by the inconsistencies which appear from the start.

The intention here is not to imply that the narrator of *La Princesse de Clèves* is in any way unreliable.[3] In the novel there is no indication that he is jeopardizing credibility, nor are there any signs of "gaming" or bad faith in the actual account of events, historical or fictional. When misleading information is conveyed to the reader by the narrator's voice, it may be attributed to the narrative point of view, fixed at the moment in question in a character who is making an erroneous assumption: the reader is merely seeing events as the given character sees them, and can readily identify the misconception, once these events unfold, as being that of the character. All instances of this nature in the novel fall well within the limits of rhetorical device (the heightening of intrigue, fidelity to characters' points of view, etc.), rather than under any rubric of narratorial bad faith.

Let us take as an example the episode of the letter which is passed to the heroine by the Reine Dauphine (pp. 1170 ff.). Mme de Clèves reads and interprets this letter under the mistaken impression that it is addressed to M. de Nemours, and the reader is subsequently treated to the heroine's conclusions concerning it:

[3] The term "unreliable" is understood in the sense in which Wayne C. Booth speaks of unreliable narrators, in *Rhetoric of Fiction* (Chicago: University of Chicago, 1961).

> Elle voyait seulement que M. de Nemours ne l'aimoit pas comme elle l'avoit pensé et qu'il en aimoit d'autres qu'il trompoit comme elle... Elle voyoit par cette lettre que M. de Nemours avoit une galanterie depuis longtemps. (p. 1172)

Nothing could be more evident than the fact that the narrator, while speaking in the third person, is nonetheless reporting the character's perceptions, misguided as they may be: these and other sentences in the passage begin with the phrases "Elle voyait" or "Elle trouvait," explicitly attributing those perceptions to Mme de Clèves. If the reader were still to entertain doubts as to the narrator's intentions, those doubts would soon be set to rest by an intrusion of the narrator's own perspective:

> Mme de Clèves n'estoit pas la seule personne dont cette lettre troubloit le repos. Le Vidame de Chartres, qui l'avoit perdue, et non pas M. de Nemours, en estoit dans une extrême inquiétude;... (p. 1173)

Far from breaching the faith of the narrative pact, this narrator is, on the whole, overtly careful that the reader have a global and reliable view of the "facts." Departures from this policy serve ends other than to lessen the narratorial reliability.

All this sets the bases of a curious narrative structure. There is a narrator who appears somewhat biased, concerned for detail, sometimes sympathetic to characters—all personal qualities. Yet there is only one explicit mention of a speaking *je*, with no other overt, concrete personal signs for this fictive construct (such as name or gender). This narrative voice tends to document the action as would a contemporaneous observer, yet there are also signs of a later chronological perspective to storytelling. The speaker poses for the most part as omniscient, but sometimes seems to abdicate that privileged status. Furthermore, this figure narrates ostensibly as a detached third person yet, while keeping the grammatical third person, gracefully switches in and out of fixed points of view of individual characters.

In short, there are inconsistencies visible from the outset.[4] Are they merely attributable to lapses in the author's memory or to quirks in her style? Such hypotheses scarcely seem plausible in light of the text's general balance and careful composition. On the other hand, could these inconsistencies be interpreted as participating in a larger scheme of ambiguity on the narrative level, a subtle pattern hidden beneath

---

[4] For treatment of similar issues in another work, see Jean V. Alter, "C'est moi qui parlons: le jeu des narrateurs dans *Francion*," *French Forum*, 5 (1980), 99-105.

a seemingly straightforward presentation? The latter hypothesis is justified by other aspects of the novel's narration to which we will now direct our attention.

II

A topic of interest to a reader sensitive to the dynamics of narrative is the question of narratorial stance, not only as it pertains to a text's implied reader, but also in reference to other textual building blocks—characters, action, setting, and the like. Evidence of satire or burlesque, in works where they are to be found, necessarily hinges upon such elements of the presentation. Of course, satire is not strange to French literature prior to, and during, the seventeenth century: the *fabliaux* and Rabelais provide a foundation on which Sorel, Scarron, Cyrano and many others build. However, we must bear in mind that the writings of Madame de Lafayette derive from quite different traditions, distant from those mentioned.[5]

The narrative voice of *La Princesse*, whatever the measure of objectivity it contains, arouses interest in its stance just the same. Obviously we are not dealing with the picaresque irony which the century's libertine or "bourgeois" novels incorporate. But it is a structure of ambiguity with ironic overtones, a structural irony, that the narrative process of *La Princesse* sets forth.

In all of this, we understand irony to be predicated upon a multiplicity of meaning to be found in a single textual phenomenon (an utterance, a structuring device, an authorial premise, etc.), customarily with rhetorical, satiric or humorous intent. Thus, to speak of fundamental irony on the level of narrative in *La Princesse* would be to postulate some sort of ironic structuring mechanism, and to imply such intent. In other words, one would need to make a case for a narratorial argument, served by a pervasive and systematic use of ironic discourse at this level. But if some narratorial pose of irony is struck, to whatever degree, it is not for argumentative or rhetorical ends that it is brought into play; rather, it is used to effect a contrast, say, between the values of the past and those of the present. In this searching sort of nostalgia, indicative of the narrator's sense of priorities, there simply is no call for the irony of satire. Irony in the novel has other faces.

[5] Cf. Moore for a treatment of the literary traditions leading to Madame de Lafayette's work.

When, for example, M. de Clèves states hypothetically that "...la sincérité me touche d'une telle sorte que je croy que si ma maîtresse, et mesme ma femme, m'avouoit que quelqu'un lui plût, j'en serois affligé sans en estre aigri" (p. 1147), the reader, along with the heroine, senses an inadvertent prolepsis. Whether the husband will later live up to this assertion becomes quite another matter which does not pertain directly to narrative discourse. This is merely verbal irony. The narrator, in the absence of argument or humor, stands apart from such verbal irony by relegating it to the voice of a character.

There is something in the narrative outlay, however, which takes on the aura of a truly structural irony, an irony of puzzlement and enigma. It is in a steady undercurrent of pessimism which dulls the glitter of a patent narratorial idealism, as we shall shortly see. Structural irony presupposes a singularity of mind which can withstand the challenge of contradictory meaning on the surface; it can go so far as to use that contradiction for preordained rhetorical ends. Such a determined constancy of position is a trait which the narrator of *La Princesse* does not appear to exemplify. But even if we were to find evidence to the contrary, ambiguities in the narrative discourse would lead us to question not so much the good faith of its presentation, as the stability of its premises. Specifically, these premises are the values which narration holds forth for society, since it is society which is the stage for the novel's action and the standard against which all ethical priorities are set.

III

From the moment a given narrator sets out to recount a story, he is to some degree involved in the recording of history. Regardless of the narration's chronological relationship with the subject matter, regardless of whether the story is true or fictitious, the speaker still appears to the reader as some sort of historian. The process is essentially the same in the *chroniques* of the Middle Ages as in the *nouveau roman*: events and descriptions are set before the reader who, if only for the sake of effecting communication, takes them to be real within the confines of this communicative circuit. Such is the nature of any narrative pact, the tacit accord whereby the narrator agrees to tell and the reader agrees to "listen." We hasten to add the explanation that "pact" may well include the telling of make-believe, or "lies," or fiction, but these can be read and taken for "real" within the conventions of a genre. Intentions of factuality, esthetics, or mere divertissement do nothing to alter this basic situation.

For the critic observing the dynamics of narration in a literary work, a primary matter of concern is then the narrator's own identifiable perspective and opinions on this "history" which is the narrative. In a novel such as the *La Princesse de Clèves*, where the setting for action is painstakingly cast in history itself, and where the telling of history becomes an element of great thematic import, this question takes on an added dimension. Yet it is precisely in this area of narratorial perspective—as concerns both the action itself as well as its historical context—that certain ambiguities can be detected.

It is understandable that action and setting would stand together in the narrator's view. To begin with, both are recorded for the novel's purposes as phenomena of the past. Beyond that, a skillful presentation draws no qualitative distinction between the historically accurate background on the one hand, and the fictive heroine's love story on the other. Thus the transition from the novel's opening passage into the Princesse's story is accomplished in such a way as to veil the reader's eye to the crossing from fact to fiction. Both appear at first glance in the glow of an idealism almost befitting a fairy tale.

This aura is achieved at the outset by the narrator's persistent use of superlatives and absolutes. The novel's very first sentence, which serves as an overall introduction for the text to follow, generalizes an air of magnificence, gallantry and brilliance for the setting in which the action will transpire: "La magnificence et la galanterie n'ont jamais paru en France avec tant d'éclat que dans les dernières années du règne de Henry second" (p. 1107).[6] Furthermore, the use of "jamais" has multiple effects: it isolates the past from the narratorial present; it reinforces the absoluteness of the descriptive terms; and, within these functions, it sets the court of Henri II in the atmosphere of a never-never land, in much the same way as a fairy tale would. Throughout the novel, the term "jamais" is used again and again in this fashion.

The opening passage goes on in the same vein, continually extolling the splendor of not only the court and the times, but of the individuals who populated them as well.

> Jamais la cour n'a eu tant de belles personnes et d'hommes admirablement bien faits; et il sembloit que la nature eust pris plaisir à placer

[6] Cf. Francis L. Lawrence, "*La Princesse de Clèves* Reconsidered," *French Review*, 36 (1965-66), 15-21.

ce qu'elle donne de plus beau dans les plus grandes Princesses et dans les plus grands Princes. (p. 1108)

...mais ce qui rendoit cette cour belle et majestueuse, estoit le nombre infiny de princes et de grands seigneurs d'un mérite extraordinaire. (p. 1108)

The Reine Dauphine is "une personne parfaite," the Chevalier de Guise "d'une valeur célèbre," the Prince de Clèves "brave et magnifique," and the Duc de Nemours is "un chef d'oeuvre de la nature." The heroine, of course, is depicted with no less enthusiasm as "une beauté parfaite," possessed of "un éclat que l'on n'a jamais veu qu'à elle" (pp. 1113-14). The accumulation of such terms, and the repetition of "jamais" in narratorial retrospect, compose in the main a view of the past as a period of perfection.

The presentation of the novel is dominated by this laudatory tone, as the narrator takes evident pride in recording such a distinguished era. This is indicative of a general opinion of the past on the narrator's part. As we have stated, the narrative discourse draws no delineation between its imaginary material and that which is historically verifiable, thus uniting the two for its own purposes under the rubric of history. Concerning the narrator as historian, we may define his opinions on the subject matter as constituting, within the narration, an attitude on history.

On the surface, this stance of admiration for the past remains constant throughout the novel. In order to convey a differing opinion, the narrator does at times fix the point of view in a dissenting character. But are there other vehicles for the expression of a view contrary to the narrator's overt glorification of the past? Is it possible that the past, in fact, represents more to the narrator than an idealized setting for action? And is it possible that this idealization, seemingly inherited from the pastoral novels of the seventeenth century, could be called into question within the narrative of *La Princesse*? Subtle signs in the narrator's own discourse suggest an affirmative answer to these questions.

Returning to the novel's opening pages, which contain the work's most concentrated historical information,[7] we find that such signs are visible from the outset. They do not mount an explicit contradiction to the general assessment of the past, but instead serve to undermine

---

[7] Valincour saw this trait in the work's beginning as a flaw, taking much less interest than we in the notion of history.

it steadily, causing the reader to wonder about the narrator's judgment. In other words, rather than establishing direct opposition on the verbal level, they seem to add a problematic dimension of depth to the apparent surface of positivity and nostalgia that seems to prevail.

The indicators to which we refer fall into three groups and, as we shall see later, their cumulative effect is reflected in still another area of the novel's narrative structure. In all cases, the inferences drawn remain at the level of the reader's response to signs which the narrator puts forth, and to the manner in which they are presented. Likewise, those inferences concern the storyteller's premises for narration (as opposed to the narrative itself), and are at implicit odds with that storyteller's explicit idealism regarding the past.

a) The first category involves what ultimately is discovered to be a pessimistic facet of the narrator's brand of nostalgia. First, it is clear (if only by chronological inference) that the narrator-historian has not directly experienced the atmosphere of "perfection" which is painstakingly portrayed. Consequently, the ideal remains a construct from the very beginning, not immediately experienced in the domain of the narrator's here-and-now. Nor does it seem likely to the narrator that this ideal could be reproduced in that domain or at any subsequent time: it is first spoken of as a fortunate and exceptional convergence of nature's positive forces at a bygone moment ("...il sembloit que la nature eust pris plaisir à placer ce qu'elle donne de plus beau..." p. 1108); and as concerns the heroine's moral "perfection," the narrator's very last words in the text make it one of a kind: "...et sa vie... laissa des exemples de vertu *inimitables*" (p. 1254, emphasis added).

One might here object that we need not read metaphysics into a text which can be interpreted as merely a fictive moral exemplum. However, if such were indeed the case, a thorny question would arise: what would be the logical point of an example which is, by the narrator's own final admission, inimitable? Quite to the contrary, the ideal serves to underscore the fictive nature of the text and, by virtue of its impossibility, to accentuate the fact that it is inapplicable to the world outside the text. Furthermore, to return to the text's world, the notion of perfection, for the narrator, remains just as it is described—an unattainable (and hence impractical) ideal which is, at best, now lost with the passage of time.

Seen in this light, the novel's first sentence puts forward an opposition which is projected over the entire narration. We have already cited this sentence as an explicit attribution of magnificence (i.e. perfection) to a particular past era: "La magnificence et la galanterie n'ont jamais paru en France avec tant d'éclat que dans les dernières années du règne de Henry second" (p.1107). In a narrative which seems to credit the king with the atmosphere of excellence at court and to attach much of its glory to his person, the use of the term "dernières années" has a clear implication: the ideal magnificence, which the narrator has singled out for explicit adulation, is already predestined to end in some measure with the death of the king. Such turns out to be the case after the enthronement of the new king: "Enfin, la cour changea entièrement de face" (p. 1219).

The opening sentence thus functions as something of a microcosmic symbol for the historical perspective of the narration: explicit nostalgia mixed with implicit pessimism. Not only is past perfection to be lamented for its loss (as simple nostalgia would have it), but perfection on the whole is doomed to extinction because of the nature of time, because of the nature of man, because of the realities with which history itself has enlightened our retrospective view. What is ultimately shadowed with a degree of doubt is not the absolute value of the ideal, but rather its practical validity. This stance in the narrator's historical perspective reflects, in turn, the conflict which runs its course in the novel's principal story, where the ideal of moral perfection is opposed by more practical and worldly concerns of sexual inclination. At this level, the ideal prevails in the end (as historical idealism is dominant in the narrator's approach), but only on the ideal plane, and not before it has undergone uncertainty through practical tests. The signs of recessive pessimism that color the narrator's speech here find their match.

b) The second area of confusion in the narrator's signs concerns the wide issue of morality, again with regard to the perspective taken on the past. It centers around the moral assessment of action on the one hand, and action on the other. With characteristic discretion, the narrator stops short of rendering moral judgments claiming to be universally true. The definition of stance is to be inferred by the reader. As Helen Karen Kaps has stated, regardless of the degree of narratorial omniscience,

> ...the narrator's comments retain a stamp of subjectivity, or personal judgment, rather than an objective norm, which invites the reader to remain somewhat detached and to form an opinion of the narrator as he does of the heroine or any other character.[8]

---

[8] Helen Karen Kaps, *Moral Perspective in 'La Princesse de Clèves'* (Eugene, Oregon: University of Oregon Books, 1968), p. 47.

The topic of morality has understandably drawn much critical attention, especially with reference to Mme de Clèves, and yet the nature of the heroine's moral system (be it bourgeois, Christian, or *noblesse oblige*[9]) is not the main point at issue. It is generally agreed that the heroine espouses the moral system set before her by her mother (pp. 1113, 1141); our immediate discussion focuses on the narrator's relationship to this system, apart from considerations of its type. In this regard, as before, a degree of disharmony must be pointed out.

One may agree with William O. Goode that the moral challenge which Mme de Chartres sets before her daughter, and which the latter accepts, is ultimately a call to distinction[10] — a goal of transcending the moral mediocrity which surrounds her, to be unlike "other women" (e.g. p. 1141). Whatever its source or motivation, it is recognized by all parties concerned (the heroine herself, the Duc de Nemours, and the narrator) as a goal of unyielding perfection well beyond the ordinary standards of good morality.

Of course, the narrator does not overtly pass a positive judgment on this code of ethics; but, since he is so evidently fond of perfection in general, it is tempting for the reader to draw affirmative inferences concerning such opinions. It should suffice to note that Mme de Chartres and her beliefs are depicted as being superior to the norm. In speaking of Mme de Chartres ("dont le bien, la vertu et le mérite estoient *extraordinaires*"), the narrator thus distinguishes her thoughts from those of most mothers in clearly favorable tones:

> *La pluspart des mères* s'imaginent qu'il suffit de ne parler jamais de galanterie devant les jeunes personnes pour les en éloigner. Mme de Chartres avoit une *opinion opposée*. (p. 1113, emphasis added)

This positive attitude of admiration on the narrator's part is reinforced by the abiding praise (if not total understanding) for the heroine's subsequent moral choices. In short, it would seem clear that the narrator views the standard of moral perfection as a positive value. Furthermore, in the absence of signs of satirical intent in narration, the

---

[9] Cf. Martin Turnell, *The Novel in France* (London: Hamish Hamilton, 1950), p. 37; also Claude Vigée, "*La Princesse de Clèves* et la tradition du refus," *Critique*, 16, No. 159-60 (1960), 728; Kaps, pp. 24-26. See also William O. Goode, "A Mother's Goals in *La Princesse de Clèves*: Worldly and Spiritual Distinction," *Neophilologus*, 56 (1973), 398-406.

[10] See Goode; see also G. Fontaine-Bussac, "L'Ethique dans *La Princesse de Clèves*," *Revue d'Histoire Littéraire de la France*, 77 (1977), 502.

greater part of the story is seen from the heroine's point of view, and she is throughout favored with admiration above the rest of society.

If indeed this code of morality is a worldly one (as I am inclined to believe), the narrator's sympathy with it is entirely in keeping with his preoccupation with society and the dynamics of the particular courtly setting. But, by repeatedly labelling both mother and daughter as "extraordinary," the narrator is demonstrating an awareness of a dramatic disparity between their morality and the amorality which permeates the court society. And therein is the rub, since that society was presented as perfect.

It involves the problem of the narrator's historical perspective on the action's setting. A striking contrast may be observed between the heroine's code of moral perfection and the reigning amorality (or immorality) at court, even though such a contrast is not directly verbalized in the narrator's speech. Seemingly unaware of the contradiction, the narrator lauds the moral ideal, yet at the same time cites the court as an arena of unequaled perfection in spite of its moral disorder. What emerges before the reader is the image of a fairy-tale variety of ideal heroine, set against an ostensibly ideal milieu which proves to be quite tarnished, but which nonetheless merits the storyteller's admiration. No outward gesture is made either to recognize or to resolve the paradox: at the same time the heroine is perfect because of her uncompromising ideals, and the court setting is perfect because of its atmosphere of magnificence. The fact that this very atmosphere is also one of moral compromise does nothing to change the narrator's assessment of it.

However, in the midst of these conflicting signs, the reader experiences no sense of disillusionment or discomfort. This may be due to the narrator's reservation of judgment. But it is also, and more probably, due to the fact that the narrative scheme makes the prevailing immorality an integral part of the setting from the very start. The first description of King Henri plays the role of a synecdochic "figure du récit"[11]: the king's extramarital relationship with Diane de Poitiers sets both the stage (for the reader) and the example (for the rest of the court) for moral permissiveness.[12] This information is conveyed in the narrative's second sentence:

[11] The term is here understood as it is used by Raymonde Debray-Genette in "Les figures du récit dans *Un Coeur simple*," *Poétique*, No. 3 (1970), pp. 348-64.
[12] Cf. J. W. Scott, "The 'Digressions' of the *Princesse de Clèves*," *French Studies*, 11 (1957), 317; also A.J. Singerman, "History as Metaphor in Mme de Lafayette's *La Princesse de Clèves*," *Modern Language Quarterly*, 36 (1975), 264.

> Ce Prince estoit galant, bien fait, et amoureux; quoique sa passion pour Diane de Poitiers, Duchesse de Valentinois, eust commencé il y avoit plus de vingt ans, elle n'en estoit pas moins violente, et il n'en donnoit pas des témoignages moins éclatans. (p. 1107)

From this point, the description goes on directly, and very significantly, to introduce the king's mistress *before* presenting the queen herself to the reader; at this juncture, and through the rest of the novel, the queen seems to exist in the shadow of the mistress, as the narrator takes more interest in Diane—symbol, that she is, of an almost institutionalized code of marital infidelity. Of her influence over the king there can be no doubt: "...elle le gouvernoit avec un empire si absolu que l'on peut dire qu'elle estoit maîtresse de sa personne et de l'Estat" (p. 1110). This affair of the king, along with all the others at court, are set forth so matter-of-factly as to show sexual immorality to be quite the order of the day in this supposedly ideal setting. Yet the narrator induces the reader to accept this situation as a simple fact of courtly life—all this in evident juxtaposition and contrast to the narrator's alignment with Mme de Chartres, the advocate of a code of moral perfection. If the narrator chooses to overlook these disparities, the alert reader surely cannot.

H.K. Kaps noticed this basic contradiction, but sees it as no problem: given the narrator's overriding fascination with the court, she judges him to be "indulgent" toward moral flaws. She also offers the explanation that the atmosphere created by such a state of affairs, constituting a "source of delight" for the narrator, could not be construed by the latter as posing a danger to the heroine.[13] Even if one were to assume this (as I am not disposed to do), such reasoning still seems to beg the question: by way of resolving the evident confusion, the reader is asked to adopt the narrator's inconsistent perspective. Instead, it is more appropriate to view this particular confusion of narrative stance in light of a broader pattern of disparity. It can be seen, indeed, with more far-reaching implications as it contributes to our understanding of narratorial perspective on history—a presentation which is positive and idealistic on the surface, yet coupled paradoxically with latent negative or pessimistic tones. As concerns the particular question of alignment with moral codes, the narrator is caught in a bind between a tolerance of compromise in a supposedly

---

[13] Kaps, p. 48.

"perfect" bygone era (an evident contradiction in itself), and the apparent acceptance of a standard which would admit no such compromise. With corroborating evidence, this points to a system of ambivalence too significant to be brushed aside.

c) The remaining area of complication in the narrator's signs is germane to the one just considered. It has to do with the coexistence of an idealistic portrayal of the court setting and the state of counterproductive political disharmony in which the court finds itself. Fundamentally the same issues can be raised, particularly the question as to how the narrator can reconcile his idealism with the flaws inherent in the political context.

Intrigues and conflicts of interest are considered in the narration as integral parts of life at court. Far from frowning upon the situation as being one of corruption, the speaker seems quite fascinated by the atmosphere which it engenders. However, in this regard (as opposed to the question of sexual morality considered above) he is at least disposed to recognize the negative implications which the reader might see: conscious of the reader's judgmental inferences, if not necessarily of his own uneven footing, the narrator makes a distinctly apologetic and defensive remark by way of reaffirming his overall approval of the court. With a single stroke of the pen, he sums up the questionable state of affairs and then adds his explicit approbation, as though he felt compelled to do so, all by virtue of the pleasant effect produced:

> Toutes ces différentes cabales avoient de l'émulation et de l'envie les unes contre les autres: les dames qui les composoient avoient aussi de la jalousie entr'elles, ou pour la faveur, ou pour les amants; les intérests de grandeur et d'élévation se trouvoient souvent joints à ces autres intérests moins importans, mais qui n'étoient pas moins sensibles. Ainsi il y avoit une sorte d'agitation sans désordre dans cette cour, qui la rendoit très agréable,... (p. 1118)

The speaker here takes a decidedly subjective approach in his judgment instead of an ideal moralistic one. In so doing, of course, he leaves in suspense the more basic problem of how this brand of "agitation" can be construed as contributing to the perfection of his utopian world, described as it is elsewhere in absolutely ideal terms. The issue goes beyond the scope of the novel's scene-setting passage (where the above-cited segment is found), as it is raised again in the passage about King Henri's death much later in the text; one notes the similarity in descriptive code, as well as the narrator's awareness that things merely appear, and are not, as they "should" be:

> Une cour, aussi partagée et aussi remplie d'intérests opposez, n'estoit pas dans une médiocre agitation à la veille d'un si grand événement; néantmoins, tous les mouvemens estoient cachez et l'on ne paroissoit occupé que de l'unique inquiétude de la santé du Roy. (p. 1216)

Again, the narrator accepts the apparent flaw as a fact of courtly life, and again, the reader may be aware of the implicit disparity between facts and opinions (or, if one wishes, between action and motif). Another such "fact of life" in this courtly setting is deception or the game of false appearances. This is of partitular interest to the narrator as it assumes a prominent place in his description of the supposedly ideal world of the past. It becomes a matter of thematic import in the action as well, since the heroine is warned about the illusory nature of appearances, and subsequently finds herself involved in the game.

We noted that Henri's extramarital affair with Diane sets a standard for the court, and that the affair plays a metaphorical role for the narrative as it is mentioned at the novel's very beginning; the introduction of the queen, even in her somewhat secondary role, serves a similar narrative function with respect to the phenomenon of false appearances. The first presentation of the queen (which is in the text's third paragraph) details some of her good qualities; the very next paragraph speaks of somewhat less positive traits underlying the surface of her appearance. After referring to her ambitions, the narrator exploits his technique of stratifying appearances and reality by raising the notion of dissimulation to the thematic level:

> ...il sembloit qu'elle souffrist sans peine l'attachement du Roy pour la Duchesse de Valentinois, et elle n'en témoignoit aucune jalousie, mais elle avoit une si profonde dissimulation qu'il estoit difficile de juger de ses sentimens, et la politique l'obligeoit d'approcher cette Duchesse de sa personne, afin d'en approcher aussi le Roy. (p. 1107)

Other characters at court follow suit, creating an atmosphere in which factions, feuds, and affairs of the heart spill over into the political arena, where they become a formidable influence. Yet through the entire text, these goings-on remain "hidden": not only (as cited above) at the occasion of Henri's death, but in general by the common practice of dissimulation. Of this the narrator is quite aware, as time and again he makes much of the pervasive game of false appearances: characters are repeatedly reported as participating in the game or falling into its traps.

But at this point one might wonder if the narrator himself has not fallen into such a trap, despite the warning which he reports as being issued to the heroine (by her mother) in the form of a maxim, illustrated thereafter by the inserted narrative concerning Diane de Poitiers. Let us not forget that the narrator shows no signs of satirical intent: on the one hand, he is caught up in a nostalgic enthusiasm for depicting the fairy-tale aspect of the historical setting, and with all attendant idealism; on the other hand, he seems blind to the implications of some less than perfect traits which underlie the setting's appearances of pomp and magnificence. But let us specify: the indicators of this kind of naiveté on the narrator's part remain for the reader in the realm of inference, to be judged by what the narrator does not say and by conclusions which he does not draw; besides this, we have attempted to show that signs of inconsistency in the narrator's historical perspective are not isolated, but instead combine to form a pattern of ambivalence. These points, taken in conjunction, now direct our attention to some other similar strategy in the novel's structure above the level of the narrator's speech. Since all signs are not immediately evident at this level, there must be another force within the text which, by its own rationale, organizes and stratifies those signs that we can read.

IV

Our next area of study is then the structuring device referred to as the "framing" of discourse — the way of arranging different levels of textual presentation. *La Princesse de Clèves* posits three such presentational levels, the most encompassing being that of the *je* in "Le libraire au lecteur," the short preface to the main narrative. This first "I" poses as the publisher and purports to speak on behalf of the author. The second source of discourse is the voice of the principal narrator whom we have been discussing. The last one is incorporated in a series of characters who, at different points, deliver secondary or inserted narratives recounted supposedly for the benefit of other characters; these stories are "overheard" by the reader as they are, so to speak, entered into the narrative record.

To this point, we have focused on the principal narrator, raising certain issues of narratorial ambivalence as regards perspective on history. In order to shed more light on this problematic area, let us now briefly consider the two other levels of discourse; in so doing, we shall note similarities and contrasts which project the problems already discussed over the entire range of the work's narrative process. At the same time, we shall undertake to situate those questions in a larger textual frame of reference; this will, in turn, provide a model (emanating from the text itself) of understanding for the apparent paradoxes now before us.

a) To engage in lengthy discussion of the function of secondary, or inserted, narratives would be an unnecessary duplication of much critical study already done. Recent analyses are in basic agreement as to the role played by this level of discourse within the narration of *La Princesse*. Stirling Haig refers to inserted narratives as "screens" or protectors which are offered to the heroine;[14] J.W. Scott and A.J. Singerman each express similar opinions.[15] There can be little doubt that stories told by other characters at least contribute to form the heroine's moral conscience, or else reflect that formation process.

There are five of these secondary narratives set within the novel, each of which deals with events prior to the time of the main action, i.e., historical accounts.[16] For different reasons, characters undertake the telling of "History," and in each case (except the first), a narrative pact is posited between speaker and listener(s). Furthermore, this narration is shown to be a valued commodity, by the listener's solicitation, by the speaker's introductory remarks, or by the thanks extended to the storyteller once the narrative is completed.

The first of the inserted narratives is the brief account by the Reine Dauphine of her own mother's (Marie de Lorraine's) misfortune in life at court (pp. 1120-21). It is told by way of apology for the Reine Dauphine's lack of influence on behalf of the heroine (the intended listener), and concludes with the storyteller's statement of concern that she will herself relive her mother's ill luck.

Next to appear is the narrative of Mme de Chartres to her daughter, about Diane de Poitiers (pp. 1129-33). It is introduced with the maxim that appearances are deceiving at the court, and goes on to relate a lesson in history whose obvious intent is to (in)form the heroine. For this storyteller as well, the past explains the present, and, in this continuum, history is exploited for didactic purposes as both past and

[14] Stirling Haig, *Madame de Lafayette* (New York: Twayne, 1970), pp. 113 ff.
[15] See references in note 12 above.
[16] Unlike most critics, we choose to include here the first story told by the Reine Dauphine, as it has all the characteristics of inserted narrative.

present are viewed as dangerous, fraught with factions and false appearances, and so on.

Third is the story about Mme de Tournon, told to the heroine by her husband (pp. 1143-52). It is introduced with an anti-feminist statement by M. de Clèves, and carries the implicit moral that appearances are misleading where the women of the court are concerned (as they excel in "adresse et dissimulation," p. 1151). It amounts to a call for sincerity (p. 1147) in a milieu where insincerity is rampant.

Following is another tale recounted by the Reine Dauphine, ostensibly to inform her listeners on the history of the English court (pp. 1161-63). She begins by offering the story of Anne de Boulen as a model of interpretation concerning Anne's daughter, Elizabeth, Queen of England. This strategy repeats the Reine Dauphine's earlier account of her own mother (see above). The story is one of jealousy and misfortune, both premised on false appearances. It relates to the heroine (who is among the listeners) through its elements of prefiguration and moralizing content.[17]

Finally there is the story, told by the Vidame, of how his own masquerading has gotten him into a compromising situation (pp. 1175-81). Threatened by circumstances, the Vidame seeks help; this particular narrative pact involves the exchange of the story for the assistance of the listener (Nemours) who, we are told, recounts it in turn to the heroine (pp. 1185-86).[18]

These secondary, framed narratives have been the subject of readers' puzzlement over the centuries, but only recently have critics recognized their proleptic and metaphorical functions. Taken together, they also constitute a solid thematic framework: all five of the stories involve some measure of jealousy, and all but the first hinge on the notion of false appearances.[19] For our purposes, they offer a revealing point of comparison with the larger "frame" in which they appear, that is, the discourse of the novel's principal narrator.

Use of the device of inserted narration in *La Princesse* differs from that in the earlier pastoral novels of the seventeenth century, where little, if any, qualitative distinction in technique separates the principal narrator from character-storytellers. In *La Princesse*, however, secondary narrators have their personal purposes and emphases as they assume the presentation. Furthermore, they set themselves apart

[17] These are detailed in Scott, p. 318.
[18] Properly speaking, the Vidame's narrative is "intercalated" rather than "inserted." For simplicity's sake we refer to the group of framed narratives under the latter rubric.
[19] Cf. Haig, p. 109.

from the principal narrator in their judgments of the historical settings in question, where the issue is once again one of perspective on history. Indeed, by virtue of the framed structure, the secondary narrators view as *present* the era which the principal narrator sees as *past*. We have already observed the latter's preponderant idealism and nostalgia in his retrospect, as well as latent signs of uncertainty. The text's secondary narrators, on the other hand, are blatantly pessimistic about their own times, contradicting the "fairy-tale" setting which the principal narrator sees fit to idealize outwardly. None of the character-storytellers shares any measure of his optimism: Mme de Chartres and M. de Clèves pose clearly as moral guardians in reaction to the dangerous environment that they perceive, and consequently tell stories with somberly didactic overtones; the Reine Dauphine sees herself ever at the threshold of danger; the Vidame's own predicament speaks for itself. They all feel a malaise in their setting and, when they recount stories from their own past, these illustrate and explain that feeling of malaise.

Inevitably we are brought around again to historical perspective. Not only is there contrast of idealistic and negativistic moods between the main and secondary levels of narration, but also as regards history itself. The secondary narrators all view the past as contiguous to their present, and history is thus offered by them as a model for the interpretation of their own society. For them, the past bears a relationship of causality with the present. For the principal narrator, however, history is largely a vehicle of nostalgia, and the past (i.e. the matter of his narrative) appears to be irretrievably lost, severed from the present, having little in common with the time in which the narrator plays historian. In short, these two levels of discourse confront the intended listener with two opposed ways of assessing history.

What we do observe here is the beginning of a structural pattern in the text's narrative scheme. At each of the two levels of storytelling, the narrator seems to be at odds with his or her own times, and turns to the past as material for narration; the difference lies, as we have said, in the assessment of the past. The principal narrator (as historian) shows his dissatisfaction with his own day only *implicitly*, setting up the court of Henri II as a point of perfection unparalleled before or since. Hence that narrator's nostalgic stance. The character-storytellers, for their part, show an explicit discontent with their own setting, and reinforce it with an equally dim view of the past, presented as the "model for the present." Such a *mise en abîme* effect in their stories, furthermore, is an expansion of a similar strategy offered in the preface entitled "Le Libraire au lecteur."

b) We choose to consider that brief preface as a part of the novel for at least two reasons: first, it appears within the novel's title page, and second, it is an obvious ploy for sympathy, hence attempting to influence the reader's opinion and to participate in the overall narrative pact.

The most telling argument, however, is that the preface's voice speaks explicitly on the author's behalf. In so doing, the *je* sets the author as well at odds with (his or her?) contemporary society:

> il a craint que son nom ne diminuast le succès de son livre. Il sçait par expérience que l'on condamne quelquefois les Ouvrages sur la médiocre opinion qu'on a de l'Autheur et il sçait aussi que la réputation de l'Autheur donne souvent du prix aux Ouvrages. (p. 1106)

The anti-historical structure is thus complete since, at each of the three levels of discourse, history is invoked only to be subsequently called into question. At the broadest level, the entire "historical" testimony of the main narrator, i.e. basically the novel, is in fact questioned already in this preface, as the authorial figure is shown to be uncertain about the relative worth of the work:

> [in reference to that author] Il demeure donc dans l'obscurité où il est, pour laisser les jugemens plus libres et plus équitables, et il se montrera néanmoins si cette Histoire est aussi agréable au public que je l'espère. (p. 1106)

Assuredly, the principal narrator proceeds to relate his story in apparent good faith, but at the same time, as we have indicated, also shows signs of uncertainty about historical perspective and morality. In addition, the novel's character-storytellers overtly take a negative view of its supposedly "perfect" setting, as evidenced in their own narratives. Finally, it is interesting to note that some degree of doubt is cast even upon the relative value of these inserted narratives: their merit is seemingly questioned, in one case, by the storyteller, and at least in one other, by the reaction of the heroine (as intended narratee). Says Mme de Chartres of her own story: "Si je ne craignois... que vous disiez de moy ce que l'on dit de toutes les femmes de mon âge, qu'elles aiment à conter les histoires de leur temps,..." (p. 1128); and further: "Je ne sçay... si vous ne trouverez point que je vous ay plus appris de choses que vous n'aviez envie d'en sçavoir" (p. 1133).

Concerning the story of Mme de Tournon and Sancerre, told by M. de Clèves: "Ce prince venoit conter à sa femme des nouvelles de Sancerre; mais elle n'avoit pas une grande curiosité pour la suite de cette avanture" (p. 1157).

But let us return to the authorial presence in the preface. Perhaps we have found here a figure within the text to whom we can credit the intent which lies behind the clever organization of signs and latent counter-signs. Why would a novel present a narrative structure designed to confuse historical perspectives in the telling of history, to show ethical ambivalence in the telling of a moral tale, and still to maintain the guise of unity on the whole? Such a careful strategy suggests the presence of a master-planner, pulling the strings, as it were, behind the scenes of the novel's narration.[20]

One plausible interpretation would attribute this plan to the "Autheur" mentioned in the preface. Depicted as uncertain of the merits of the work to follow, this master-planner would thus mirror the uncertainty in the novel's narrative scheme. In that sense, this scriptor would adopt the purpose of defining the text *not* as history, philosophy, or ethics, but specifically as *fiction*, i.e. the one form of prose writing which needs not answer to the demands made of rhetorical discourses. Just as Mme de Chartres declares, "Si vous jugez sur les apparences en ce lieu-cy,... vous serez souvent trompée" (p. 1129), perhaps the "Autheur" is delivering a similar warning about the ontology of the novel: it may appear to be history, it may appear to refer to reality with its historical processes, but appearances are deceiving in the world of fiction which has its own conventions of writing and reading.

V

Focusing on the narrative strategy of *La Princesse*, we have isolated two problematic areas for consideration: narratorial perspective and the framing device of the work's overall presentation. Questions have arisen which afford no simple, formulaic solution; nonetheless, at least a tentative conclusion is in order.

Any attempt to arrive at an understanding of a novel's narrative plan should properly take two issues into account: generic conventions and the global literary context of the period. With regard to the

---

[20] To meet charges of intentional fallacy, let us point out that we refer not to the intentions of Madame de Lafayette the woman, but to those of a scriptor whose signs may be seen within the text.

former, we know that the "historical novel" enjoyed popularity in France during the second half of the seventeenth century.[21] One could thus be tempted to ascribe the narrator's historicism to a mere desire to please the public's taste. Yet we must remember that the story's historical setting is neither neutral nor inert, since characters interact constantly with it; furthermore, as we have shown, historical perspective manifests forcefully the narrator's presence in the novel. Still we must avoid the opposite extreme of reading *La Princesse* as a historical document. Jean Boorsch has pointed out that, aside from its imaginary content, the narrative abounds in inaccuracies and anachronisms when compared to the true history of the late 1550s.[22] Obviously "history" means something other than "History" in this text.

Consideration of the period in which the novel appeared, the classical era of French literature, is no easier. Critics have long been sensitive to the classical elements in *La Princesse*, not the least of which is the Jansenistic predetermination of events.[23] While other traditional tenets of classicism have been noted in the novel, one attribute—harmony—which seems to figure in every critical description of the period, poses a problem in reference to *La Princesse*. Obviously classical harmony cannot account for the disparities that we have seen in the text's narrative scheme. Thus, there must be something in the novel's organization which transcends its period, relating to the dynamics of literature in general.

What are our indicators? The telling of the story shows concurrent signs of overt idealism and latent pessimism, holds forth a moral exemplum proceeding from an uncertain ethical basis, and displays a multiplicity of narratorial roles. The net effect of such an intriguing structure is to divert the reader's attention from the world outside the text, and to focus that attention on the world within the text. What text is it then? It poses intermittently as history, exemplum, memoir and psychological study—yet no single one of these can serve to define it. The reader can sense that he or she is being invited, *gratia artis*, to view a world in which fact is contiguous to fiction without transition, a world which can assimilate the various thematics and modes of discourse.

---

[21] The popularity of the historical novel in the second half of the seventeenth century is noted by Antoine Adam, *Histoire de la littérature française XVIIe siècle*, IV (Paris: Editions Domat, 1954), pp. 161-64.

[22] Jean Boorsch, "Madame de Lafayette and the Manipulation of History," *American Society of Legion of Honor Magazine*, 46 (1975), 105-09.

[23] Kaps, p. 24.

This invitation constitutes the narrator's part of the narrative pact by which he agrees to tell a tale and, in the process, to entertain or instruct. Indeed the tale is told in scrupulously linear fashion, but at the same time, ambiguities abound—ambiguities that cause the reader to reevaluate and redefine the narrative pact. In any literary work, such signs which direct attention toward the internal dynamics of the text function as the first step in a textual self-definition. The reader of *La Princesse* is confronted with a system of ambiguity in narrative perspective and posture. He or she can either ignore it or take it into account. To ignore it would be tantamount to rejecting much of the premise of narration. To include it in reading, the reader is first constrained to ask: who is this multi-faceted, enigmatic narrator? The answer can only be: the narrator of a *novel*, that literary form which creates its own world for both story and storytelling. And beyond? Having accepted the text's self-definition along with the resultant conventions and modes of reading, the reader has begun to uncover a subtle system of pessimism which has far-reaching effects in the text's meanings.

In addition to ontological evaluation implicit in the text, another key to understanding the narrative structure lies in the treatment of history. Regardless of its source, real or imaginary, most of the narrative material falls here under the rubric of history. But not only are the past events in themselves important; so is their telling. If nowhere else, this is made manifest in the narrative framing device through which the telling of history is integrated in the plot. As for the characters, they have their own reasons that compel them to speak of the past. For the narrator, history is a source of material as well as an occasion for a perspective on the past. And for the author in the preface, "histoire" is the book itself. In all cases, history is something more than the picture of the past. It takes on added dimension as a model of interpretation, within the action, and a force which initiates and directs the novel's narration.

At issue here is ultimately the notion of judgmental perspective. The narrator's interests define his values. Whatever contributes to the air of magnificence and intrigue bears intrinsic worth for his storyteller's vision; he is caught up, along with his characters, in the game where appearances are deceiving. The thematic of moral perfection is also set in relief, but a curious double standard undermines its position. Finally, history and narration themselves prove to be of great value. Here the multiplicity of roles played by the narrator, each with its different time setting, forms a composite image which subtly underscores the narrator's own fictive status and, far from abstracting him completely from the story, makes him an inherent part of its development. Yet, what helps the narrator to elude precise definition is the fact that, at the same time, a narrative distance is necessarily imposed by the mode of historiography in retrospect, the mode chosen as the overall vehicle of presentation.

For the moment, before we turn our attention to this dynamic of distance, it is the opposition of idealism and pessimism in narratorial (i.e. historical) perspective which will occupy us, and with good reason. Conclusions pertinent to the nature of the novel's narrative scheme are to be found in this avenue of inquiry. If the narrator's words are the glass through which we view the text's fictional society, what we see is a double image, at once favorable and unfavorable, which we should examine closely before passing beyond.

2. The Gaze of History

Historical perspective in *La Princesse de Clèves* is marked by the paradox of idealism and pessimism. This duality underlies the narrative scheme, but of course is less an overt thematic opposition than a latent ambiguity. That it provides the tone and initial premise of narration comes as no surprise; beneath the serenity of a positive attitude, there flows a current of doubt. Even if it is only implied, the disappointment in the failure of the ideal is all the more disturbing because the narrative itself places so much stock in that ideal.

The principal problem, as noted earlier, stems from the narratorial perspective which detects, or rather, creates a moral gap between the background and the characters whose actions are set against that background. The narrator is very much set on idealizing the times, but his enthusiasm flags significantly with regard to the characters who populate those times. In other words, the characters, in their human imperfection, cannot live up to the "perfection" of the era.

This attitude involves some far-reaching implications concerning both human nature in general (in the purview of the narrator-psychologist) and historical perspective of narration (narrator-historian and narrator-memorialist). Inasmuch as the narrator's attitude bears not only upon characters of an isolated historical time, but on characters who manifest much more general human traits, the narrative accordingly constitutes a commentary on human nature. On this score, characters perform poorly in that they are unable to transcend frailty and, so to speak, to rise to the occasion—that "occasion" being the idealized times which the narrator has abstracted from the rest of history. Despite the convergence of all sorts of positive factors—perfection of ancestry, worldly fortune, chance, and even physical appeal—the characters still find themselves limited by the human condition. If all is not well at court, if the most positive values are not the ruling order, and if all is not for the best in this best of all possible worlds, then something inherent in human nature must be responsible for the imperfections that preclude a fairy-tale ending in a fairy-tale setting. Again the question arises: why create a myth, only to animate it with characters and action which, far from being mythical, are caught up in the more earthly concerns of human existence?

One way of answering the question would be in suggesting that an idealized, mythical setting serves to stress by contrast the pessimistic judgment rendered on human nature; indeed, human nature in the text is generalized and certainly not confined by narratorial perspective to the reigns of Henri and François II. The implicit judgment is of course that human nature is tinged, if not dominated, by its weakness, both in the idealized setting of the historical/fictive narration and in the period which we may call the *narratorial present* (i.e. the period which has come to be known as "le Grand Siècle").

The issue of the "historical situation" of the narrator must thus enter into the question. The fact that human nature is put to the test in so pointed a fashion indicates that it is not merely the character of the Princesse, or of the society surrounding her, that is being scrutinized by the narrator; the indication is instead that much of the narrative material actually transcends the setting which is so painstakingly depicted, in order that more permanent and atemporal values and issues may be examined. Yet we also remember that much of the action, and many of the values which the narrator calls into play, are in large part those of the seventeenth-century society. Thus the interpretation of historical perspective would have to take into account the fact that both human nature in general, and seventeenth-century values in particular, are being projected upon a mythologized, if relatively proximate, past. This is the primary manner in which the novel's historiography views its material, the way in which it begins to organize the "past" which it describes/invents. And that past must indeed be considered a disappointment for a narrator who begins his story by extolling its virtues.

The part of history which is imaginary in the novel (that is, the love story of the Princesse) falls short of the narrator's ideal because the heroine's desire for perfection makes her incompatible with her society. Therefore it proves to be an unworkable or impractical value. As concerns the genuine history (or the documentary/historical information conveyed in the narrative), it too is a disappointment because that society does not live up to the promise of perfection which the narrator holds out for it from the very beginning of the text.[1] Both disappointments appear under the same aegis of narration.

In *La Princesse*, a parallelism exists between these two facets of history-telling, and it is borne out in the characterization of the heroine. She and her mother (whom we may consider as an extension of the heroine on the ethical plane) are the only characters who make the notion of uncompromising perfection a matter of thematic import, and who subsequently endeavor to live by its code. Interestingly, they are the only two principal figures in the text who are of an entirely fictive nature. In this light, the heroine may be viewed as a product of fantasy set against a genuine historical background; the fantasy, however, is unable to survive in society, and that society (portrayed in line with historical documentation) likewise proves to be incapable of eliciting perfection in its members.

To take the issue further, there appears to be a degree of uncertainty in the way the narrator's historical situation appears. This uncertainty has to do with the very meaning of history and with the place in history attributed to the narrator's own century; theoretically perfect, yet undermined by suspicions of inner corruption, disintegration, and more specifically (or in a fashion more pertinent to *La Princesse*) by the question of the inherent imperfections of the human condition, perhaps fueled by the Jansenistic approach to the ontology of man.

The times, despite the trappings of glory and the semblance of harmony, turn out to be less stable than they appear at first glance. This point, however, applies not only to the setting for the novel's action, but also (by implication, it would seem) for the historical situation of the narrator himself.

We have already noted that the novel's king has in effect two wives; we have also noted the confusion which this fact causes in the social priorities at court and in the resulting atmosphere of factional rivalry. In addition to this difficult and potentially volatile situation, we see that the hierarchy within the nobility at court is not clearly defined.

---

[1] See Ann M. Moore, "Temporal Structure and Reader Response in *La Princesse de Clèves*"; also "History and Temporal Structure in *La Princesse de Clèves*," *Proceedings of the Eighth Annual Meeting of the Western Society for French History*, 8 (1981), 131-46. Both articles treat the relationship between the two time schemes.

For example, Diane de Poitiers is virtually as powerful as a queen; the Guise brothers are raised to the level of *pairs du sang* at the funeral of Henri II; and the social stock of individual characters at court rises and falls in line with factions or faction politics. Eventually, the accession of the new king (pp. 1219 ff.) entails an important social realignment in the court.

As for the narrator's historical situation, we know this period (i.e. the latter part of the seventeenth century) to be one of social turmoil as well. It is an era in which society finds itself grappling with the growing influence of the bourgeoisie, and with corruption and political disunity within the nobility. Given the somewhat analogous situations of turmoil in the setting for the action of *La Princesse* on the one hand, and the socio-political climate of the times of the text's composition on the other, the assumption may be made that there is some correlation to be seen between the disappointed optimism of the narrator vis-à-vis the text's society, and a similar (if only implicit) disappointment with the narrator's own "Grand Siècle." Besides, the process of history itself must amount to a disappointment to the narrator: even if the past *were* perfect both in setting and in *personae* (which it is not, as the narrative turns out), that perfection would have been lost to the times of the narrator who views in retrospect the splendors of a bygone century.

It appears, then, that narratorial pessimism in *La Princesse* is a reaction to three problems; frailties of the human condition, the instability of the times (past and present), and the disappointing nature of history. This pessimism is exacerbated by its structural opposition in the text with a much more evident idealism. Paradox is evident in this point, and is indicative, at the same time, of a deeper and more general pattern of ambiguity which raises important issues of understanding for the novel's reader.

What manner of historiography, what mode of historic narrative can base itself on such an antithesis of idealism and pessimism? This question alone will become an important issue as we attempt later to categorize the narrative presentation according to historiographic standards. However, the matter goes further for, inherent in this narratorial dualism there is an almost overriding concern for the *forms* with which history writing deals: outward social forms are observed in this fictional society, but in the absence of concern for inward ideological consistency with those forms; of key interest to the narrator, then, is this system of forms and the qualities in the heroine which set her apart within that system. Our assessment of the novel's narrative/historiographic strategy will have to take into account this attitude on forms, and at the same time, we find ourselves drawn back to the problem of defining the characteristics of our narrator/historian in light of his coexisting idealism and pessimism.

II

How are we to integrate the paradox of idealism and pessimism into our reading of the text? And what are we to make of that wide disparity between the supposed greatness of a "Grand Siècle" and the moral malaise of characters and secondary narrators who function in that very setting? It is, after all, that same sort of disparity that vexes the principal narrator in his own century of greatness. Furthermore, what are we to understand from the marked incongruities in the novel's action—incongruities which seem to bear a structural relationship with the text's narration and implicit (or explicit) moral codes?

The more evidence of paradox and incongruity we accumulate, the more widespread and significant these elements appear to us in the text's composition. In order to include into our reading of the text this signifying process—one which is sown deep into the novel's structure—we are forced to attribute it to (or, at the very least, affiliate it with) the narrator's own implicit premise that perfection, happiness, and harmony cannot coexist with stability in society.

In other words, it is clear that, throughout the novel as a whole, the ideal remains an unattainable goal; efforts to implement this ideal are repeatedly frustrated in the unfolding of the action, and the ideal, because of its loftiness, remains an abstraction for those who are cast in the earthly plane. The role of the narrator in all this is complex: first, he is the *porte-parole* of the novel's master planner, but he also shows an awareness, through hindsight and imagination, of how things might have been; by the same token, his view of history is colored, as we have shown, by his consciousness of the necessary gap between the ideal and the real in all things. Hence a predetermined pessimism in the telling of the story, emanating from both historical perspective and a more general and atemporal view of the human condition. A comprehensive integration of the text's overall idealism/pessimism paradox must take this attitude into account. Seeing this basic principle beneath the general organization of the text, one can then make consistent sense of other ambiguities related to the notion of the failed ideal.

One problematic area in this regard is found near the end of the novel, where the heroine refuses her final chance for earthly happiness (now permissible under even extraordinary earthly ethics) with the Duc de Nemours. Many a reader, persuaded by the overwhelming idealistic fanfare and by the rest of the elements of fairy tale, will find the heroine's final commitment disconcerting, if not unnecessary.[2] However, if one takes into consideration the narrator's pessimistic thesis that perfection is incompatible with the fulfillment of human design, the Princesse's refusal becomes perfectly integrated with a fundamental, if latent, premise for the telling of the tale. The final denial of happiness on the part of the protagonist thus represents the logical and necessary conclusion drawn from the opposition between a pessimistic foundation and a more evident, yet textually ineffective, idealism.[3] The text, it may be said, draws its logic from paradox, from the unresolved confrontation of idealism and pessimism.

In this light, "reasonable" explanation is also found for a germane and equally problematic aspect of the text, that is, the justification which the heroine offers for her final decision. She cites two principal reasons: first, that her code of moral perfection prohibits her from profiting by her husband's death—a development for which she scrupulously accepts a share of the blame; second, that Nemours, having once attained his goal of possessing her, would tire of her and would allow his affections to stray (pp. 1247-48). Each reason offered is somewhat incongruous because, for the first, a strong case can be made for the heroine's innocence, and, for the second, such an assertion about Nemours contradicts everything that the reader suspects (optimistically, as the evident tenor of the narrative would have it) of the character's attributes, based on what has been said of his remarkableness up to that point in the novel. But, of course, neither of these two justifications is without ideological root in the context of the seventeenth century. The first, which is an appeal to absolutism in morality, is mirrored in the virtually contemporaneous *Phèdre* of Racine[4] and in the overall moral system underlying all of his tragedies (perhaps as an influence of Jansenism). The second of the Princesse's reasons is a typically classical and Cartesian dim view taken of the

---

[2] Consider the conclusion of Corneille's *Le Cid* where honor, the play's major motif, is set aside for Chimène by royal edict in favor of love.

[3] See Claude Vigée, and also Francis L. Lawrence.

[4] According to Racinian morality, Phèdre's affections are guilty even after the news of the supposed death of Thésée, because that which is wrong is thus predetermined and invariable.

appetitive aspect of love.[5] But within the bounds of this novel (or, perhaps, to retain only the overtly suggested reference for reception, i.e. the fairy-tale sort of reading model), both of these explanations raise questions, since they both betoken an ideological stance that perfection is not an earthly attribute — and in that world whose "perfection" supposedly inspires the narrator. In the final analysis, the incongruity must then be cited as the actual working out of the pessimistic premise which we have identified as the narrator's latent thesis.

There is also the scene of the *aveu* — the single event in the novel which has provoked the most controversy in interpretation, and has been criticized over the centuries by the work's detractors for its entirely paradoxical nature. The reading of this scene in the perspective of narratorial pessimism affords an answer to such criticism. To the charge that the scene is too unrealistic to be believable or to fit in with the rest of the action and setting, one need only respond that realism or truth-likeness are beside the point if the *aveu* is in keeping with a larger pattern of ambiguity — a pattern predicated on pessimism throughout the text.

In other terms, the assertion that the heroine's confession to her husband violates principles of *vraisemblance* is actually a call for a logical explanation of what motivates her to take this extreme measure. There can be no better logical explanation than that of a consistent premise of the novel's composition, by which the quest for perfection necessarily finds itself at odds with social convention at every turn. For the pattern that brings about the confession is the very same one which systematically prefigures the failure of the ideal in society. Beyond that, the criticism is also an appeal for an optimistic conclusion harmonious with the rest of a supposed fairy tale. Our point is that the fairy tale's foundation, not outwardly evident, calls into question the possibility of perfection surviving along with happiness.

Charges of *invraisemblance* aside, the other criticism of the avowal scene deal with the set of values that prompt the heroine's speech: while it is true that sincerity is at least supposed to be an absolutely positive value, how could the heroine be so naive as not to foresee the deleterious effects of her candor? The answer to this question again draws on the notion of a general pattern which constrains the heroine

---

[5] This particular attitude, of course, dates back well beyond Descartes to Plato, whose earlier and most evident proponent in seventeenth-century France was d'Urfé in his *L'Astrée* and *Epitres morales*.

to confess, and at the same time brings about effects which are directly opposite to those that she had intended. The Princesse's ethical system insists upon her sincerity, and yet that sincerity is ill-fated from the start in a society where relationships are permeated with false appearances, deception, and insincerity. If sincerity meets necessarily with misunderstanding, it is because that sincerity forms a facet of a code to which society is inhospitable.

III

The notions of predeterminism and pessimism, on one side, and history, on the other, are very closely joined throughout this novel. We have already cited the work of others with regard to the proleptic aspect of past events (i.e. the events anterior in time to the material of the principal narration, as well as this material itself once it constitutes a past for the heroine): in that regard history functions as a model for the very composition of the novel. On the level of action, the Princesse looks to history as a model of interpretation, putting her knowledge of history and her own personal past to the task of guiding her present life. On the level of narrative, history becomes the primary source of inspiration: the principal narrator makes it his business to construct a "historical" narrative; and of course character-narrators make their own recounting of past events the material for intercalated narrative. In these ways, the influence of the *past* upon the *present* is made manifest. In all these senses, it is the past which dictates the present of events, the heroine's reactions to these events, and even the organization/telling of those events in the narrative record.

Therefore it is proper to speak of the intertwining of history and determinism in the novel. History functions doubly as the chronicle of past events, as well as the exponent of predetermined fatality. At the same time, it is important to recognize that no such concept of historical predetermination in seventeenth-century France could have occurred in a vacuum. Whether Mme de Lafayette was of Jansenist persuasion is somewhat an immaterial consideration. The fact is that the notion of predestination of souls and events is very much a current one in the 1670s, and that it is very much in tune with the rationalistic philosophy of a fixed order of the universe, the ideology which carried the day in that century's thought.

Certainly it is a common motif in classical literature, especially tragedy, for the past to determine the present. The entire moral code underlying the tragic universe of Racine is predicated on the principle that history and fate are functions of each other.[6] The issues in question are thus an intransigent moral code, as dictated by history or the past, and the phenomenon of predetermination, detected in the role which the telling of history plays in the unfolding of the novel's action. These are two integral components in the Jansenist world view, and together they are of capital importance to the composition of *La Princesse*. H.K. Kaps calls attention to the connection with Jansenist principles[7] but, given history's role as it becomes more and more significant before our eyes, especially with regard to morality and fate, it would seem that the matter deserves more than a passing mention. The point is that the functions of history (on the levels of both action and narrative), as well as the development of the heroine's moral code, have in common a basic premise that is remarkably similar to that of the Jansenists.[8]

The issue goes further, though, since history takes on a progressively greater dimension as a determinant factor in the novel. Its functions of prolepsis and interpretive model on the plane of action are familiar to us, as are its implications on the level of narrative; but it also participates in the construction of the crucial, intransigent code of morality. Morality becomes inextricably joined to this foreshadowing variety of history inasmuch as that history is recounted to the central character with didactic intent, and contributes greatly to the formation of her conscience and ethical system. In this respect, history functions not only for the reader, but for the heroine as well, and not only as an interpretive model: in the case of the intercalated narratives recounted to the heroine, history is held before her as something of a challenge, a standard to live up to, a lesson of past calamities to be avoided. Efforts to rise to that challenge are made as the Princesse refers her judgment at every turn to the moral dicta of her mother and husband—dicta which take on in her eyes the proportions of ancestral conscience not dissimilar to that of the sun in *Phèdre*.[9]

[6] See Eléonore M. Zimmermann, *La Liberté et le destin dans le théâtre de Jean Racine*, Stanford French and Italian Studies 24 (Saratoga, Calif.: Anma Libri, 1982).
[7] Helen K. Kaps, p. 24.
[8] In reference to the functions of history in the novel, see also Pierre Malandin, "Ecriture de l'histoire dans *La Princesse de Clèves*," *Littérature*, 36 (1979), 19-36, and also A.J. Singerman.
[9] Jean Racine, *Phèdre* (Paris: Larousse, 1971), lines 1242, 1273-77, 1310, among others.

All of the sides of historical perspective that we are discussing—proleptic, fatalistic, pessimistic, and virtually ancestral—are reflections of one another. Nowhere is this more evident than in the parallel roles played by the Princesse's mother and husband. First Mme de Chartres informs her daughter on events from the past, then, after having observed and judged her daughter's conduct, she delivers a stern moral lecture from her deathbed, following which "Elle vescut encore deux jours, pendant lesquels elle ne voulut plus revoir sa fille,..." (p. 1142), underscoring the importance of a message which precedes her death by some days.[10] M. de Clèves, for his part, imitates the actions of Mme de Chartres very closely, as he delivers his own didactic history concerning Mme de Tournon, after which he too observes and draws inferences upon his wife's conduct, and finally pronounces the same sort of moral sermon from his deathbed, whereupon "Il languit néanmoins encore quelques jours et mourut enfin..." (pp. 1236-37), without any further word reportedly addressed to the heroine, as if again to imply that his moral statement need be his paramount message to the Princesse.

In the end, the heroine accepts the moral standard, together with its attendant historical model. Exercising her ethical choice, she patterns her conduct after that of both her mother and husband. After delivering something of a moral discourse to M. de Nemours by way of explaining her final refusal, she retreats into a silence which remains unbroken until her death, explicitly rejecting all direct communication with Nemours. History, seen in this light, plays the many roles which we have attributed to it: it furnishes the material for both levels of narrative, but as present events themselves become past, they constitute another kind of history that serves subsequently as a moral determinant and moral model, as well as a model for textual structure. The fatalistic basis of pessimism is made manifest at each step of the way, since the underlying message and motivation at each point are indeed a "tradition du refus" (cf. Vigée), a persistent call to renounce the illusory ideal of happiness in this life.

Criticism of *La Princesse* has pointed out the classical nature of the principal conflict within its central character, i.e. the opposition of

[10] This silence on the mother's part does not contravert the conclusions of John D. Lyons in "Narrative, Interpretation and Paradox: *La Princesse de Clèves*," *Romanic Review*, 72, No. 4 (November 1981), 391. But it does pose some interesting questions in light of his remarks on silence in the novel.

reason and passion.¹¹ This is indeed the main dilemma for the protagonist, as one might expect of a classical heroine. And, as one might further expect of a novel in which historicism is a prime constituent of both narrative and motif, history plays an important part in the progression of this central opposition. Each of the inserted narratives, or "histories," deals thematically with a similar conflict of reason and passion. In that context, history-*telling* moves Mme de Chartres to become a force of conscience and reason. History is both communicated to the heroine with didactic intent, and later viewed by her as model (even though a negative one) and justification for her moral choices.

IV

The relationship which history bears to religion and matters of conscience is as characteristically complex as it is subtly nuanced in the narrative. While it is a principal contributor to the heroine's system of ethics (on the level of motif) and is the mode of expression for this ostensibly moralistic story (on the level of narration), yet history in all its forms appears separated from religion. In fact, certain critics have stressed the aspect of the "morale laïque" on which the protagonist's system is founded.¹²

Kaps attempts to refute this argument of a non-religious morality by citing the fundamentally Christian values upon which the Princesse's ethics are based, along with other seemingly Church-centered activities in her life.¹³ This counter argument would be more compelling were it not for one fact: the narrator, who is sympathetic to the heroine, and whose moral assessments the reader is likely to accept, refrains from linking the heroine's choices to any Christian source of obligation; furthermore, the supposed chronicle shows no overt metahistorical signs of religious thesis or affiliation. On the contrary, the positive ethical system is narrated into the novel without metaphysical basis before our eyes or before those of the narrator.

Let us consider the narrator's spatial perspective on the central character. While it is true, as Kaps observes, that the Princesse seeks refuge in a "maison religieuse," the important fact is that the narrator's

---

[11] Cf. Lawrence, p. 15; also Charles Dédéyan, *Mme de Lafayette* (Paris: Société d'Edition de l'Enseignement Supérieur, 1955), pp. 188-97 (as cited by Lawrence).
[12] See Martin Turnell, p. 137, and Vigée.
[13] Kaps, pp. 24-26.

vision does not follow her into that place.[14] This narrator is habitually omniscient, yet such an absence of the heroine from his sight (while she is at the convent) seems to indicate that, in this case, he adopts society's perspective on her: while she is hidden from society, she remains hidden from the narrator. Despite the narrator's laudatory tones in depicting the Princesse's outward quest for perfection, this fundamentally social (as opposed to "religious") outlook would correspond to a social, rather than religious, basis for her moral choices. For the narrator follows her everywhere else she goes, in society and in retreat; yet he acts here as if he had no access to her thoughts while she is cloistered from the world — and this cloister constitutes her sole explicit contact with the institution of religion. While she is so sequestered, the narrator reports of her only what her intermediary reports to Nemours (p. 1253). To state the issue from the opposite point, one may also note that this atypical (in narrative terms) sojurn in the "maison religieuse" is the narrator's *only* mention of religious significance in his heroine's life: nowhere else does he even mention Church, prayer, or theology, though the occasion would logically present itself many times.

Finally, to the same extent that the narrative avoids the issue of religious spirituality for the protagonist, it also steers away from the socio-religious institution of the Church and from Church history. No association is drawn between Church and State, virtually no mention is made of religious affiliation or practice within the court (except for Marguerite's Protestant ties), and indeed religion is an inert issue in the narration of the main action. Even the Cardinal de Lorraine is spoken of only in his socio-political capacity in the world. From all of this we can infer that the term "laïque" applies not only to morality in the novel but also to history and to the narrative's historical perspective.

V

How do history and historicism affect the reader? The opening few pages of the novel have, over the centuries, had the tendency to put readers off, and this primarily because of their historical-documentary nature. A.J. Singerman cites the first published study of *La Princesse*, whose author (probably Valincour) states: "En lisant cette longue description de la cour, je crus que j'allais lire l'*Histoire de France* et

[14] Kaps, pp. 24-26.

j'oubliai la *Princesse de Clèves*."[15] The remark by Valincour is most *à propos* in that it shows the reader at work, explicitly in the process of defining the nature of his activity. And Valincour's implicit question could very well be our own. From one vantage point, our impression is that we are reading a chronicle of the sixteenth-century French court, at least as far as the illusion engendered by the narrative pact is concerned. From another perspective, however, we are alert and informed readers, taking note that we are reading a novel, i.e. that much of the material is fictive and that the text as a whole is constructed, narrated, indeed governed, by the principles and conventions of novel writing, even if the novel should create the illusion of being a historical documentary.

At this point we may stress the distinction between the two concurrent levels of reading at which we approach a historical novel, or any conventional novel, for that matter. In our more general approach to the text, we view it as a novel and read it as such, all of which implies the critical perspective on literary and imaginative writing. The other level is a more restricted and contingent one where the reader's field of vision is limited to the make-believe tenets of the narrative pact. In this perspective, the reader accepts the illusion that he is reading history—regardless of the veracity or the imaginary nature of narrative. This is of course a distinction which could be discussed in reference to any narration of past events that are "supposed" to be real, and indeed most novels fall within such parameters. But the historical novel, *La Princesse de Clèves* included, complicates the issue as it introduces documentary and verifiable information in historiographic fashion, and proceeds under that aegis to narrate fiction without effecting any modal transition between the two subject matters. Thus the reader's two perspectives can cross (or actually coincide) and, like Valincour viewing the text within the confines of the narrative pact, we may ask ourselves if this is indeed history or fiction that we are reading. The question is more pertinent here than in the case of a more conventional novel (say, one of Flaubert) for the reasons that we recognize elements of historical reality in the narrative, and that we recognize the rubric and technique of historiography; in other words, our understanding of *La Princesse*, our assessments and reading performance, all are influenced or even conditioned by our prior experience with historical texts.

[15] Cited by Singerman, p. 261. See also Antoine Adam, *Romanciers du XVIIe siècle* (Paris: Gallimard, Bibliothèque de la Pléiade, 1958), p. 57 and endnote.

Ultimately the novel is playing on this convergence of levels, this neighboring relationship, and is overtly calling on us (by virtue of the relationship of resemblance, the metaphor of textual modes in which novel mimics history) to read it as a historical document. Again, this is insofar as our reading is dictated by the terms of the narrative pact. In *La Princesse*, the illusion is reinforced by the evident fact that history/documentary constitutes the reader's initial contact with the work. The opening passage sets the stage for historical narrative, and by the same token, it defines the overt modal relationship between the narrator and the reader. History thus furnishes the bond which joins narrator and reader in the contingent narrative pact. And there is no presentational signaling device, no change in narratorial voice, at the point where the documentary ends and the fictive love story of the Princesse begins (p. 1113). On the contrary, the latter begins with the phrase "Il parut alors une beauté à la cour,..." with the term *alors* bridging any gap of logical sequence. Sequence is at the heart of the question as we endeavor to arrive at a working description of the literary workings of (pseudo)historiographic discourse: the narrative beckons the reader to cross such a bridge as the present *alors* that joins the parallel shores of discursive modes; as a rule, the transition is a subtle and smooth one because narrative voice will not call attention to it, and the reader may (choose to) accept the illusion.

Critics of historical novels often dwell on the dynamic structural relationship between the fact and fiction therein. The question which ordinarily arises is: to what extent does the former determine the latter in the text's scheme of composition? The issue hinges on the role of history with respect to the way in which plot is organized into a basic frame for the narrative. For *La Princesse*, the matter need not be raised on the level of authorial organization, but rather on the level of motif.[16] There history is a model for action, serving as a thematic force: characters, rather than author, consult history and react to it, feeling its subtle and determining influence. As for any determinant effect of history in the actual composition of this novel, we have already had the occasion to note that, once the heroine is first introduced, fiction overshadows fact despite the continuity in presentational technique.

The narrative pact, which is no more bound by extratextual rules than any other element of *novel*, would have the reader take the entire work as historical. This is of course the illusion created by the

---
[16] See both articles cited above by Ann M. Moore.

narrator's voice, and that illusion is maintained through to the end of the novel. The narrator's ostensible role is that of historian, even though there are other important facets of his presence (discussed in the preceding chapter). Given these circumstances, history is seen to make up the narrator's principal and most evident link with the reader. Whereas, for the author mentioned by the "Libraire" of the preface, the pseudohistorical presentation constitutes the novel, and for the characters, history constitutes a model (or at the very least, a means of divertissement), it is for the narrator and reader the bond that makes possible the telling of the tale as it is.

All of this affords a somewhat exalted status to the telling of history in this novel. Standing out in relief, history-telling alerts us to its importance on the thematic level (in the absence of blatant signs to this effect in the narration), and thus calls our attention to metahistorical dynamics in narration. Then questions come to mind that bear on history's contribution to the narrative process and its self-awareness in that process. What indications does the "historical" story-telling give of itself? What kind of historiography dominates the telling of the tale? What interpretations are suggested by the manner in which it is told, and in what ways may this "history" be classified?

VI

Our study of the dynamics of history in *La Princesse* must involve, at this point, some categorization of the historical process that is in operation in the novel's narrative, apart from extratextual concerns for veracity and the like. We proceed from the premise that, with respect to discursive mode, the reader of this text is dealing with some manner of historiography. This being the case, our goal should be to make our assessment of it inclusive, in order to account for both the chronicle aspect of this "historical" novel and the broader historical aspect of the text as a narrative of past events assumed to be real under the terms of the narrative pact. Aside from offering the obvious benefit of further qualifying our understanding of such areas, this endeavor will help to classify the historical perspective taken by the narrator (again, if only within the assumptions of the "pact"), along objective parameters inductively attained from the broader study of historiography.

By the same token, it will furnish a reliable extratextual point of comparison for observations on the status and nature of history within the text. This does not contradict our previous assertion that the novel need not be held accountable to the world outside its own writing. On the contrary, we intend to study the very illusion which it consciously puts forward as it takes advantage of its "neighboring relationship" with true history. In other words, we are merely accepting as a working hypothesis the make-believe of the narrator's stance as historian. If, in so doing, we find a means to confirm traits already attributed to the narrator, it will be through the use of an independent mechanism which is applicable to the novel's narration and does not lead us afield in our limited scope.

A suitable methodology for this undertaking is offered by Hayden White in the introduction (subtitled "The Poetics of History") to his *Metahistory*.[17] These ready means of describing and dividing historical processes incorporate a comprehensive system equipped to treat the particular material at hand, namely an intricate narrative plan in a historical novel. While it is true that White's own study deals with history-writing in nineteenth-century Europe, his approach—with some very superficial modification—can be applied to any writing of history, even the writing of fictive history.

After distinguishing between *chronicle* and *story*, the latter amounting to chronicle (the simple representation of events, according to White's terminology) complemented with elements of plot and motif, White proceeds to distinguish further among three principal modes in the conveyance of historical information: the mode of emplotment, the mode of argument, and that of ideological implication. These are the standards intended to serve as comprehensive delimiters for the classifying of all sorts of history writing. The application of the criteria associated with these categories to the actual writing of history in a given case enables one to identify and describe, by group and by tendency, the process of the historiography in question.

The first key means of categorizing a historical document relates to the interpretive device that is built into the text by virtue of the manner in which the material is presented. The kind of story that is to be told offers, by its very nature, some degree of explanation of the story's meanings and the point of view from which it is narrated. For various reasons, White adopts the nomenclature developed by Northrop Frye in his *Anatomy of Criticism* for the codification of

[17] Hayden White, *Metahistory* (Baltimore: The Johns Hopkins University Press, 1973), pp. 1-42.

archetypal plot constructions.[18] One of the modes of historical emplotment which corresponds very closely to the presentation of *La Princesse* is

> ...fundamentally a drama of self-identification symbolized by the hero's transcendence of the world of experience, his victory over it, and his final liberation from it—the sort of drama associated with the Grail legend or the story of the resurrection of Christ in Christian mythology. It is a drama of the triumph of good over evil, of virtue over vice, of light over darkness, and of the ultimate transcendence of man over the world in which he was imprisoned by the Fall.[19]

This is the mode which White refers to as the Romance.[20] This particular organizational technique would seem to be used in the novel since it is, by White's analysis, paradoxically pessimistic as regards the human condition. Redemption (or, in this case, the attainment of the ideal) is possible, but only through the transcendence of the human condition; and idealism is set in opposition to pessimism regarding the world. Such is indeed the case in *La Princesse*, whose heroine must sacrifice all in order to attain the "new order."

White goes on to cite Romance as the historic genre which signals "...the emergence of new forces or conditions out of processes that appear at first glance either to be changeless in their essence or to be changing only in their phenomenal forms."[21] This seems to refer directly in *La Princesse* to that which we have labeled the "proleptic" role of history, that is to say, the tendency of historical events to prefigure future events. On the surface, on the level of human reactions, history does repeat itself; nevertheless, through those repetitions and the heroine's resulting acceptance of the historical model,

---

[18] Northrop Frye, *Anatomy of Criticism* (Princeton: Princeton University Press, 1957), pp. 158-238. White explains: "The principal criticism of Frye's literary theory seems to be that, while his method of analysis works well enough on second-order literary genres, such as the fairy tale or the detective story, it is too rigid and abstract to do justice to such richly textured and multi-leveled works as *King Lear*, *The Remembrance of Things Past*, or even *Paradise Lost*. This may be true; it probably is. But Frye's analysis of the principal forms of mythic and fabulous literature serves very well for the explication of the simple forms of emplotment met within such 'restricted' art forms as historiography" (p. 8).

[19] White, pp. 8-9.

[20] It is to be understood that, although Frye's terminology refers to literary texts, the same is used by Hayden White as a descriptive taxonomy of historiographic functions. This is to say that we are not necessarily typifying the novel *La Princesse de Clèves* as a Romance plot structure, but rather that we are referring to the emplotment of past events in the narrator's historic perspective.

[21] White, p. 11.

she does achieve in the end some sort of transcendence, even though it is one which brings on her death and necessitates her refusal of happiness.

The other three possible techniques of historical emplotment are not applicable, and may be quickly discounted. Certainly the text does not show comic vision; nor can it be called Tragedy since, according to White, the tragic view of history portrays the resignation of man to the conditions under which he must function in the world; finally, the text could not qualify as Satire (despite its pessimism) because no structure of satirical irony exists, as we had occasion to note in the preceding chapter.[22]

White's methodology next includes an explanation of historical presentation by criteria of formal argument. This second level of conceptualization addresses the form which a historical interpretation takes. The standard of classification here deals with different metahistorical presuppositions about the matter of history, different basic ideologies or world views. One of the four paradigms offered is that in which "...the depiction of the variety, color, and vividness of the historical field is taken as the central aim of the historian's work."[23] However, in this particular conception of perspective,

> ...the uniqueness of the different agents, agencies, and acts which make up the "events" to be explained is central to one's inquiries, not the "ground" or "scene" against which these entities arise.[24]

This "Formist" mode of explanation seems particularly appropriate to the narration of *La Princesse* because the narrator clearly sets his goal as the representation of the color and vividness (i.e. the *éclat*) of the courts of kings Henri and François II, yet also accords a place of high priority to the uniqueness (even "strangeness") of the protagonist in her social situation. At the same time, the Formist historian "...may be inclined to make generalizations about the nature of the historical process as a whole."[25] Such is again certainly the case, as we have seen from our previous findings concerning narratorial perspective on history in the novel. In short, the presentation of *La Princesse* illustrates this Formist mode of explanation in its narrator's perception of the historical field and in the demarcation of his interests

[22] White, pp. 7-11.
[23] White, p. 14. White acknowledges his basis in S.C. Pepper, *World Hypotheses: A Study in Evidence* (Berkeley and Los Angeles, 1966), part 2, pp. 141 ff.
[24] White, p. 14.
[25] White, p. 14.

and priorities. But this also accounts for the narrator's great concern for *forms*, the observation of outward social forms within the fictional society and the nature of the forms themselves.

As before, the other paradigms offered by White's categorization of formal argument can easily be eliminated. *La Princesse* could not qualify as Organicist because it is neither reductive (depicting the particulars in the historical field as parts of a synthetic process), nor teleological; likewise it cannot be called Mechanistic since it does not seek to deduce the laws which govern the operations of history; finally it could not be labeled Contextualist, for the protagonist is so much at odds with her context as to be atypical of it — her morality, along with the course of her activities, cannot be explained by anything in her milieu, her choices are without historical precedent, and the narrator draws attention to these facts.

The final step in White's methodology of classification deals, as one might logically infer, with the present time of narration and with the storyteller's relation to, and beliefs about, that present world. In this area we would look for a rubric to accommodate the narrator's obvious nostalgia for times past, as well as his malaise with his present time as compared to the idealized facets of the past. Now, White's four "ideological positions," in their general titles, appear anachronistic and perhaps inappropriate to our particular needs, since, directed toward the nineteenth century, they distinguish between Anarchism, Conservatism, Radicalism and Liberalism. On the other hand, White himself notes that

> ...the terms "Anarchist," "Conservative," "Radical," and "Liberal" are meant to serve as designators of general ideological preference rather than as emblems of specific political parties. They represent different attitudes with respect to the possibility of reducing the study of society to a science and the desirability of doing so; different notions of the lessons that the human sciences can teach; different conceptions of the desirability of maintaining or changing the social status quo;[26]

If we then were to replace the terms by the actual descriptions of those attitudes, one does indeed suit the situation of *La Princesse*. Through it, historians are

> ...inclined to idealize a *remote past* of natural human innocence from which men have fallen into the corrupt "social" state in which they currently find themselves. They, in turn, project this utopia onto what is

[26] White, p. 24.

effectively a non-temporal plane, viewing it as a possibility of human achievement *at any time*, if men will only seize control of their essential humanity, either by an act of will or by an act of consciousness which destroys the socially provided belief in the legitimacy of the current social establishment.[27]

This "Anarchistic" attitude is fitting to the narration of *La Princesse* as it denotes the narrator's view of his present society as well as that of the proximate past (tainted, as we have shown, by a partially negative opinion), yet it accommodates the speaker's non-temporal nostalgia for a "perfection" which is out of step with both chronological settings mentioned. Finally, the heading also encompasses the narrator's latent brand of pessimism. Thus, the category in question is appropriate, while the heading may seem improper: perhaps the term "anti-social" would serve the present purposes better than "anarchistic."

We could arrive at the same classification by eliminating the other models. None of the other proposed ideological stances applies to the narration of this novel; it cannot be said to be Radical or Liberal because it envisions no future utopia; nor could it be characterized as Conservative because it does not extol the institutional structure which currently prevails (i.e. the status quo of the seventeenth century in France).[28]

There are two obvious advantages of such a recourse to a reliable taxonomic system. First, it provides us with a concise and methodical means of classifying and situating the historical (both documentary and fictional) discourse of the narrator; in other words, it furnishes an inclusive checklist for drawing up an inventory of signs pertinent to his role as historian. Second, it allows us to make use of the established scholarship of historiography as a means of verifying the validity or accuracy of our findings. Although this is primarily a taxonomic exercise aimed at categorizing the narrator, the process of classifying does shed light on narrative functions by comparison to the larger extratextual and synchronic study of the writing of history.

To summarize these findings:

— *La Princesse de Clèves* qualifies as historical discourse despite complicating aspects of narrative voice, and, by affinities with other historical writings set in the same modes, certain traits of the narrator may be interpreted, not as anomalies, but as functions of the historical perspective adopted;

[27] White, p. 25.
[28] White, pp. 22-29.

— in historiographic terms, the pessimistic undertones are logically consistent with the mode of emplotment;

— this emplotment has a logical thematic correlative in history's tendency to foreshadow itself in the novel's action, or in other words, historical prolepsis (already linked as a classical *topos* to determinism) is also consistent with the archetypal emplotment of the historical discourse;

— the "Formism" of the argumentative stance offers another justification for the inexorable character of the heroine's actions (again, by objective measures of historiography), invoking "laws" of social, or in this case, anti-social causation;

— the narrator has a historian's ideological perspective (i.e. nostalgic, non-temporal utopian, hence somewhat pessimistic), even if the presence of this perspective in the novel's narrative is problematic and difficult to interpret, and even if it does not divide society or have a corresponding thesis that is overtly argued on the thematic level;

— the particular combination of modes which we have attributed to the narrator (regarding emplotment, argumentation, and ideological implication) makes sense historiographically, and in fact it matches one of the basic modal homologies postulated by White.[29]

Having arrived at this point, we are ready to move on to a consideration of the field of history-telling itself. We shall proceed first with the area that sparks the keenest interest in the narrator and actually sets parameters for the telling of the tale: the text's fictional society and the social climate in which the narrative's events unfold, that splendid and corrupt circle which fascinates the narrator yet which the heroine comes to reject.

[29] White, p. 29.

3. Society: Sight and Sound

I

Historicism in the novel, along with the overall phenomenon of history in both its matter and its telling, all of the manifestations of the novel's complex historical process, share a common goal of curiously crossed purposes. Through the sustained and multi-faceted historical discourse of the novel, there are two apparent effects, one standing in contradiction of the other. Apparently serene in the contemplation of the past's supposed perfections, the narrator-historian uncovers an inevitable corruption there. But the anomalous nature of this standoff between idealism and pessimism portends no further resolution than to be subsumed by a larger pattern of ambiguities. So, we set aside this weighty issue in order to deal with "history," treating it as a force within itself, as though its direction were not divided. In other words, let us speak of it for the moment solely as the telling of past events, either those which have bearing on the characters and action, or the broader set of events which constitute the material of the novel's narrative.

Careful appreciation of the many-tiered and nuanced historical process in *La Princesse* accords it exalted status in our reading. First, and in most general terms, we realize that history provides the narrator's *raison d'être*. Also, the narrator is recognized as being not at all disinterested in history as a metaphysical force or as a thematic in his narrative. By the same token, critical study of the novel has revealed the considerable metaphorical function which is served by history, rendering it a model for narrator, characters, and action alike.[1] This is a complex structure of history, to say nothing of the idealism/pessimism opposition that makes it all the more perplexing at every level.

Let us understand the term "action" to denote that which French critical parlance calls *fable*. The ways in which history prefigures or even predetermines events recounted in the action will become clear as we investigate certain elements of emplotment. But the complex narrative structure makes it possible for history to function on virtually every level of the text's composition: not only does it pose both as background and principal story for the narrator, but it also bears great interest in the heroine's mind, and eventually assumes a determinant role in her deeds; as a process it even becomes part of the action where its communication provides activity for the characters. Still, in regard to its determinative power, it must be said that history goes one step beyond its metaphysical role of mirror to the action or thematic outlay, and actually takes a hand in the outcome of the action, concentrating its power in and around the society it serves. The immediate goal of this chapter will be to demonstrate this dynamism of history in the novel's action, that is, the backdrop of events which antecede that action, as well as the historical vision of the heroine which kindles in her the need to represent and to re-present the past.

Even in light of the text's overriding preocccupation with the recording/telling of past events, and despite the lofty status and great influence of historicism, the recording of history would be little more than an empty gesture if it had no context in which to function, no frame of reference to which it could contribute meaning or from which to derive its relative meaning. Such a frame of reference is provided by the social setting in *La Princesse de Clèves*, the intriguing society of the court. In the complex historical vision that the novel sets before our eyes, it is this society which is both the subject and the object of history. Characters conscious of the past's hold on the present join forces with the narrator whose interests and values are rooted in the past, and the result is the "historical" novel which we read. And at the center of each of the many levels of historical perspective encompassed, we find the court society under scrutiny—or more specifically, the particular issue of morality as defined or practicable within (but not by) that society.

---

[1] See Alan J. Singerman.

In the centuries since the publication of the novel, there have been, as one might expect, many critical attempts at breaking the action down to a basic quest or central conflict. The most common such reduction has justifiably focused on the heroine's effort to reconcile her peculiar morality with the supposed real world in which she finds herself immersed at a tender age.[2] One has little difficulty in isolating this as the principal action since the heroine's greatest conflict is of a psychological nature and since moral judgment obviously has to do with the rectitude of her chosen course of action. From within the first few pages of the novel until the climactic final encounter with Nemours and the heroine's definitive refusal of earthly happiness, the reader's attention is almost constantly riveted either on the interior conflict itself or on the implications which outer events have on that conflict. *Whether* the heroine succeeds in her effort toward making her ethics and the "real" world compatible with each other is a matter for the novel's closure; *how* this effort proceeds is the main material for the novel itself.

Such are the artistic advantages of the text's chosen narrative scheme in which the technique of fixed point of view creates further illusions within the narrator's discourse. The narrative is thus composed largely of the record of the protagonist's perceptions, communicated almost directly (via the technique of narrative point of view) to the reader. The added advantage is that those perceptions convey information not only on the development of moral conflict, but also on the nature of the social milieu which, in part, necessitates that conflict. Given this, shifts in narrative point of view from the heroine to other characters are most revealing: they reverse the process by relating complementary information, specifically, society's perspective on the heroine. As concerns the reader (and by extension, the narrator), society is not exclusively the hostile setting; it is also the interested observer, able to offer *its* interpretations of the protagonist. This occurs at points throughout the text, and most significantly toward the end where crisis leads to decisions affecting important figures in society. Perceptions of the Vidame and Nemours, for example, bear on the heroine's character and furnish other points of reference according to which she can be assessed; certainly this form of reference is important if the novel is to portray effectively the dynamics of the social context. An abiding narratorial interest in that society is a very good indication that the matter is of significant priority in the novel's scheme of things.

[2] See Martin Turnell, Claude Vigée, and Geneviève Fontaine-Bussac.

The text's final perspective on the heroine, however, is that of the narrator himself. Departing from the predominant fixed point of view, the narrator speaks for himself at the end, as if to assume a vantage point above both the heroine and society. This closure technique enables him to imply endorsement of her choices. But even in closing, the narrator refrains from overt judgment, suggesting the deduction that it is the opposition between individual and society which necessitates the anti-social (hence pessimistic) dénouement.

For the heroine, then, life is a divided existence. This could not be more obvious in the spatial disposition of the action which alternates between seclusion and society. On the one hand, seclusion values the ideal which, regardless of its sources, presumes all along a superhuman or transcendent moral code; by itself a supposed dedication to sincerity takes it beyond the conventional understanding of morality; finally in this respect there is the set of positive morals and the call to distinction which is set before the heroine.

On the other hand, there is the sophisticated world of everyday usage, the real world of human frailty, insincerity and compromise—in a word, the world of life in society. The unfortunate, but immutable, fact is that the two sides cannot be reconciled. Since by its nature the call to distinction cannot integrate into society, the heroine's effort to join the two is predestined to fail. This is still another indication of a latent, yet determinant, pessimistic model for the composition of the novel's action and narrative.

In the preceding chapter, we spoke of a narratorial attitude toward history, darkened with a degree of pessimism; there it was stressed that pessimism is resultant of the reality of time. But at this point in our study, the implicit pessimistic conclusion may also be seen to stem from the reality of society, that is to say that the aristocratic society as portrayed in *La Princesse* embodies certain intransigent codes which ultimately drive the heroine into seclusion in her quest for *repos*.[3]

II

There can be little doubt from the beginning of the novel that attention will focus solely on the upper echelon of society. Representatives of the middle or lower social castes are very few indeed: apart from an occasional valet, the narrator's only other mention of a non-aristocrat is that of a bourgeois, the Italian jeweler; even with this

---

[3] Cf. Simone Fraisse, "Le 'repos' de Madame de Clèves," *Esprit*, 29 (November 1961), 560-67.

lone appearance, the narrator does not spare a passing tilt at this merchant's visible success, saying that

> Cet homme... s'estoit tellement enrichy dans son trafic que sa maison paroissoit plutost celle d'un grand Seigneur que d'un marchand. (p. 1114)

This is enough to convince one of the narrator's keen interest in society in general, and of his great concern for social register and appearances in particular.

For the rest, the characterization is drawn from the nobility. This selectiveness is so comprehensive as to offer evidence of a link with the tradition of classical tragedy, as far as characterization is concerned. As a result of this kind of presentation of an insulated aristocracy, no serious challenge of the prevailing social order could be mounted from outside the noble class. Interestingly, and despite a rather firmly entrenched code of hierarchy within that class, the only effort toward modification of the social order comes from inside its own ranks.

This social circle leads a highly codified existence, but the code, for all its pomp and order, is still subject to some question. Theoretically, at least, power and influence emanate from the king and queen, and are exercised in varying degrees, according to social rank, by the *pairs du sang* and the lesser nobles. Further hierarchies are in place within the individual families of the latter groups. Lastly, the Church hierarchy has token representation in the person of the Cardinal de Lorraine, but only as an extension of the hierarchy of birth since this character is a member of one of the noble families. Upon this fixed order which is based on birth, considerations of politics are superimposed.

The order of influence in the society is carefully drawn and supposedly unbending: higher nobles give what amount to orders to lesser nobles, everyone shows deference to "Madame," the king's sister, and so on. Nonetheless, and in conjunction with a careful presentation of social hierarchy (as though by contrast), there is a tacit challenge to the tenet of intransigence. First, we noted above the disarray in the mirroring of the king's extramarital relationship with Diane de Poitiers, as well as the resultant erosion in the queen's standing, all of which is made plain at the very beginning of the novel. The issue goes further still; in a society that relies heavily on visual symbols, delineations are crossed as lower members take on the outward signs of higher rank while some of loftier birth see their fortunes fall. The narrator documents with great detail the rise of the Guise brothers, for example, and gives witness to the importance of the visible social signs such as the carrying of the king's robe at the royal funeral (p. 1219). The affairs of state are likewise caught up in matters of personal politics, as is the case with the fate of the Connestable. Finally, the positive values of sincerity and personal integrity are sacrificed in an atmosphere highly charged with political and romantic subterfuge. The result of all such workings within the supposedly fixed social order is a system of signs which, while coherent and consistent at first glance, proves to be an unreliable system of communication because of its shifting basis: there are gaps between some characters' genuine and assumed social/political status; similar gaps exist between most characters' genuine priorities and their outward behavior, as virtually all figures are in some measure prevaricators in their social dealings; in social or personal terms, characters' outward signs can (and often do) convey meanings which run contrary to a preordained order; and through it all, the narrator shows no concern over the confusion, and the characters merely accept it as a fact of life for the most part.

What stands out here is the point that, in spite of the supposed nobility of all the characters, and in spite of expectations that noble characters be indeed worthy of the title, some games are played with truth in communication. Outward signs of perfection belie an inner frailty, for individuals as well as for the society on the whole, and consequently the great network of social relationships is not as stable within as it appears on the surface. Scarcely a conversation is reported in which some participant does not dissimulate true intentions or reactions. Nowhere is this more the case than in respect to love relationships, and the implicit message therein is that there is a predestinately poor system of signs for the communication of love within the text's society.

In fact, language and other conventionalized signs prove to be so ineffectual that the only reliable signs turn out to be the non-verbal ones: compare, for example, the awkward plea of M. de Clèves for the affections of the heroine in conversation (p. 1123) to the much more effective visual communication which characterizes the first meeting of M. de Nemours and the Princesse (pp. 1126-27). Through the rest of the text the pattern is borne out, where language is cumbersome and ineffective in crisis and tension, while the true marks of love are read in involuntary or unspoken reactions: even the *aveu*, one of the few sincere, spoken admissions of true sentiment is not intended for the object of love, but only overheard by accident; to make matters worse, it misses its mark with the husband, and ultimately causes great confusion. Nemours, for his part, is forced by *bienséance* to speak in discrete, codified formulae during his few private meetings with the Princesse, and words are of little avail in his courtship of her. He is obviously much more effective as a man of action and daring, one who proceeds directly, with few words, toward his goal, "stepping over chairs" if indeed necessary, as we see him upon his introduction into the narrative. Thus, a pessimistic message can be read in the novel's depiction of conventionalized, codified sign systems which are shown to be insufficient after all.

One sees emerging a pattern of "behavioral masks," means used in society to disguise true intentions and to project a false image of characters' motivations. Unreliable signs and symbols beset communication in many areas, but especially as regards love: the heroine's words to Nemours, until their last meeting, can never be relied upon to represent her true feelings; the episode of the Vidame's intercepted letter (an instance of written and concretized language) serves to underscore the misleading nature of the verbal sign, while a visual sign, like a facial reaction, is much more true to its meaning.[4]

The contrast between the verbal and the visual seems clear in light of the entire episode of the Princesse's portrait, commissioned by the husband and stolen by Nemours. Great value is attached to the concrete visual image, as is the case with concretized language in letter form. But the difference is in the symbolic worth of the sign when weighed against its communicative effectiveness. Since the visual sign performs a more direct, non-semantic process of reference, its value is beyond question and characters rely on it. The verbal sign, on the other hand, calls for interpretation to break its code. As interpreters, the characters show skills that are inconsistent, prey to the passions and to jealousy, and hence language is devalued.

Like the portrait, the visual (i.e. non-verbal) sign serves as a token of exchange. In the episode of the theft, the event is carefully narrated in terms which convey the importance of vision and visual exchange on the part of the principals:

> Mme de Clèves apperceut... M. de Nemours,... et elle vid que, sans tourner la teste, il prenoit adroitement quelque chose sur cette table.

---

[4] See Peter Brooks, *The Novel of Worldliness* (Princeton: Princeton University Press, 1969), pp. 71-77, for an insightful discussion of the visual and the gaze of society in this novel.

> Elle n'eut pas de peine à deviner que c'étoit son portrait, et elle en fut si troublée que Mme la Dauphine remarqua qu'elle ne l'écoutoit pas et luy demanda tout haut ce qu'elle regardoit. M. de Nemours se tourna à ces paroles; il rencontra les yeux de Mme de Clèves qui estoient encore attachez sur luy, et il pensa qu'il n'estoit pas impossible qu'elle eust vu ce qu'il venoit de faire. (p. 1164)

Mme de Clèves herself attaches significance to the visual image which again serves as token ("Ce qu'avoit dit Mme de Clèves de son portrait luy avoit redonné la vie en luy faisant connoître que c'estoit luy qu'elle ne haïssoit pas," p. 1198) and as a reliable sign that is set *en abîme* for Nemours (Nemours is watching as the heroine "...s'en alla, proche d'une grande table, vis-à-vis du tableau du siège de Metz, où estoit le portrait de M. de Nemours; elle s'assit et se mit à regarder ce portrait avec une attention et une rêverie que la passion seule peut donner," p. 1227). Finally, the value of the visual image is enhanced by the fact that efforts to carry over the dissimulation which typifies verbal exchange meet with markedly less success, as witnessed by the number of times when characters are unable to control their facial (i.e. visible) expressions.[5]

III

Consideration of the thematic of the visual in *La Princesse* brings to mind one obvious area of comparison with the tradition of the pastoral romance, most alive in the earlier part of the seventeenth century. I refer specifically to games of masking which are conducted on a general basis, and for that generality are accepted as "real" or verisimilar by the reader, again as a fundamental tenet of the narrative pact. Disguises in the pastoral tradition of course involve the hiding of true identity and the establishment of a system of false identities. Obviously, such is not the case in *La Princesse*. But the peripatetic nature of physical disguise in pastoral or *précieux* literature is replaced in some measure by a similarly functioning behavioral mask in *La Princesse*— not one which obfuscates the vision of the reader or of the wary character-observer, but one that is necessitated by social convention to the point where it is a function of codified discretion. Likewise, it is not a mask to alter the identity of character, but rather it alters the society's perception of the character's role. While the signs

---

[5] For a somewhat different assessment of verbal and non-verbal communication in the novel, see Christian Garaud, "Le Geste et la parole: remarques sur la communication amoureuse dans *La Princesse de Clèves*," XVIIe Siècle, 121 (1978), 257-68.

of character remain intact, qualities of candor and ingenuousness can be significantly changed in social dealings. Such events are common in the narrative:

> Mme de Chartres vit dans ce moment pourquoi sa fille n'avoit pas voulu aller au bal; et, pour empescher que M. de Nemours ne le jugeast aussi bien qu'elle, elle prit la parole avec un air qui sembloit estre appuyé sur la vérité. (p. 1137)

These illusions can take the form of verbal ambiguity and dissimulation as with the Duc de Nemours:

> Mme la Dauphine... demanda à ce prince ce qu'il disoit à Mme de Clèves. S'il eust eu moins de présence d'esprit, il eust esté surpris de cette demande. Mais prenant la parole sans hésiter:
> —Je lui disois, madame, répondit-il, que l'on m'a prédit que je serois élevé à une si haute fortune que je n'oserois mesme y prétendre. (p. 1160)

The heroine herself often plays the game: "Mme de Clèves ne faisoit pas semblant d'entendre ce que disoit le Prince de Condé; mais elle l'écoutoit avec attention" (pp. 1135-36); she also feigns illness in order to avoid an embarrassing situation no fewer than six times through the novel—though other characters often know better of her hidden intentions. In a word, she plays the game poorly: "Ce luy estoit une grande douleur de voir qu'elle n'estoit plus maîtresse de cacher ses sentimens et de les avoir laissé paroître..." (pp. 1169-70). She is no match for the society around her as she attempts to dissimulate visible signs, since it is reported at least fifteen times throughout the novel that her uncontrollable facial expressions are (or would be) perceptible to others.

The game of visual deception in *La Princesse* differs in graphic proportion from the far less subtle system of physical disguises in the baroque pastoral tradition. Only a general comparison can be drawn here between the highly sophisticated game of behavioral nuance in *La Princesse* and the broader game of identity change in *L'Astrée*, for example. However, each in its respective context arises from, and plays upon, a flawed or insufficient sign system. In the pastoral, disguise is more actively embraced by characters who are in search of a communicative device of *rapprochement*, since language and the conventionalized signs of love are sufficient only to cause misunderstandings. In *La Princesse*, dissimulation is a reaction, a necessity brought on by the rather bourgeois ethic of maintaining appearances; it is further caught up in the fact that society places scarcely any value at all in the notion of marriage for love, relegating love to a secondary or tertiary role in that uniquely social institution and thus inviting characters to engage in deception for love's sake; finally in all this, society sets discretion as a higher priority than sincerity in the later novel.

These differences aside, the baroque novel and *La Princesse* show a similarity in the depiction of the individual in society who feels the constraint to adjust the conventional sign system. Likewise, both portray social settings in which there is a distinct tendency toward the compounding of problems in the interpretation of social signs—compounding problems by the introduction of duplicity and masked purposes. The tendency begins at the level of the individual, where characters experience a private, personal need for things to be different. If the individual must disguise his behavior, it is because circumstances do not favor honesty, and for the moment at least, it becomes a question of how the *moi* understands itself and society.

IV

It is Claude Vigée who initiated the study of the *moi* in *La Princesse*, expanding the study of its derivation to include not only consideration of the *précieux* (and Cornelian) tradition, on the one hand, but also the opposing Racinian and Jansenistic ontology of the individual, on the other. Vigée's compelling assertion is that the *moi* in *La Princesse* is caught between two polar concepts:

> l'oeuvre de Corneille et celles des écrivains précieux expriment une morale idéaliste et humaine, axée sur l'individu triomphant, doué d'une liberté à la mesure de son estime de soi, que les jansénistes abhorrent. On trouve dans Racine l'incarnation d'un naturalisme désespéré, — véritable nihilisme à l'égard du monde, — dont les solitaires de Port-Royal sont les partisans... *La Princesse de Clèves* est l'expression du conflit irrésolu entre ces deux conceptions de la nature humaine, et, jusqu'à un certain point, une tentative désespérée de concilier leurs antinomies. D'où le malaise qui nous saisit à la lecture de ce livre ambigu.[6]

The fact that the novel is shown by Vigée not to participate wholly in either one of these two traditions lends support to the arguments of A.M. Moore that the text's organization derives from another source as well (namely, the epic), and that *La Princesse* uses a combination of Racinian and Cornelian thematic techniques.[7]

---

[6] Vigée, pp. 724-25.
[7] Ann M. Moore, "Temporal Structure," pp. 566-68.

If we consider each of the four areas upon which Vigée focuses his attention (i.e. the literature of the *précieux*, Corneille, Racine, and *La Princesse de Clèves*), we find that the conflicts which constitute the principal action are essentially the same: some variation on the opposition between love and duty. In each area or text mentioned, however, it is found that characters react differently to that opposition. Corneille and the *précieux* writers depict a dynamic of *amour/devoir*, as well as a situation for that dynamic, which are diametrically opposed by the later Racine and the overall Jansenistic perspective; engaged in an ill-fated effort to reconcile these two views is the action of *La Princesse de Clèves*, situated in the middle and sharing wholly in neither while participating in both. As we attempt to define the concept of society in *La Princesse*, shifting the center of attention from the *moi* to the level of society, we shall reach conclusions strikingly similar to those of Vigée concerning the individual.

Central in all cases is society's moral standing, its position with respect to whatever constitutes the prevailing moral code. It comes as no great revelation that the question of moral choice is of the highest importance not only to the classical hero, but to his baroque counterpart as well. Where the two visions differ is in the implications of the symbolic moral role played by the society in each case. In Racine's tragedies, society stands as the silent judge (corrupt as a worldly entity, but recognizing absolute values), the final arbitrating force on earth. Of course, society is not present to the action, but it symbolizes, standing, as it were, behind the action, and exercising some constraint on that action which we see on the stage.[8] In that invisible society, as well as microcosmically on the stage, social order is not in doubt because it always remains a metaphysical absolute despite characters' efforts to change (i.e. realign or reinterpret) natural priorities. In this way, the society behind Racinian tragedy functions more as a force than as a presence, having the role of the absent and morally concerned judge.

In Corneille, too, the society incorporates a great value, but its moral code is far less present before our eyes and remains something of an abstraction next to more immediate (humanist) considerations, such as concerns for the stability of the kingdom in *Le Cid*.[9] Society is thus presented as more of a political entity than a moralistic one, preoccupied with problems of human dimension.

---

[8] Consider in this light *Andromaque*, lines 1586-92, *Bérénice*, lines 376-80 and 729-34, and in *Britannicus*, all the mentions of "Rome."
[9] See line 1254.

In literature of the *précieux*, as a function of the difference in length and in genre, conflicts are set in the context of a society whose dynamics are much more visible to the reader than in the works of either Corneille or Racine. As would be the case in Cornelian perspective, society must interpret an abstract morality—hence the role of druids and oracles in pastoral romances. And again, central problems are socio-political in nature (e.g. honor and status of the family, communication in love relationships, etc.), while moral issues remain at the level of refined interpretation (e.g. the debate on the nuances of love, the quest for a consistent ideological foundation, etc.).[10]

One may succinctly state the fundamental differences in the conceptual organization of society between Racine and the Cornelian/*précieux* corpus of literature by saying that, in the case of the latter, society is loved and protected by its gods, whereas in the case of the former, society is the safeguard of the moral system dictated by angry or unsympathetic gods.

Where does this leave us? The point to be made is that *La Princesse* is again situated between Racinian and Cornelian derivation, now as concerns the conceptualization of society. From the Jansenist position, the depiction of social context would be portrayed as somewhat transcendent; society, in absence, embodies the absolute morality preordained by the gods, and in comparison to which the individual is predestinately guilty. Such is not the case in the present novel. In a contrary, *précieux* perspective, there would be a humanist presentation (or understanding) of society as a political entity, either grappling with problems defined in terms that are of human proportion, or applying human reason in the interpretation of a transcendent moral order. This model does not fit the novel either.

Set apart from these two is the text's concept of society, blatantly portrayed as quite amoral, leaving the individual (specifically, the heroine) in a void to define her own absolute code. As we have seen, her only points of reference in this quest are history itself, and conscience which is scarcely anything other than a function of history. This is to say that a moral code does not make itself manifest from anywhere outside the heroine's social context: morality is, first and foremost, a code of social proportion and terms, comprised of social markers and consequences, as the heroine inherits and perceives it. Thus, what

---

[10] See Laurence A. Gregorio, "Implications of the Love Debate in *L'Astrée*," *French Review*, 56, No. 1 (October 1982), 31-39.

remains from the Jansenistic side is the atmosphere of guilt (i.e. according to her own accepted code, the Princesse is still guilty of complicity, illicit passions, compromise, etc.), while there remains a humanist presentation of society caught up in human concerns, but devoid of the consistently idealistic tenor of the baroque/Renaissance stance. Something is incorporated from each of the opposed currents, setting the novel's derivation of social concept between them.

In terms of historiographic perspective on society, then, *La Princesse* indeed occupies middle ground between two polar traditions, lending support to the finding of a pervasive undercurrent of pessimism throughout the novel. Society, like the *moi*, is set forth in an ontological bind, committed to the impossible task of reconciling ever divergent conditions of existence. The impossibility of the endeavor does not speak encouragingly for the situation of either the individual or the society.

V

Despite widely varying interpretations of the novel's general meanings and of the heroine's psychology and motivation in particular, there has been, since the work's publication, a surprisingly broad common ground in the critical understanding of the social context which it sets forth. Critics from Valincour to those of the present have recognized that, first, the novel restricts its social setting to the court, and also that this setting is unmistakably portrayed as the arena of danger and controversy for the protagonist. They are likewise in unanimous accord that society counts for much in the course of the novel's action, that it interacts with the heroine as a crucial force hostile to her moral system, regardless of the origins of the latter.

Critical discussion of history in the narrative never wanders far from the topic of social context. Students of the novel have generally been sensitive to the fact that the narrator plays social historian as much as any other role. But this narrator, even in his function as simple storyteller or memorialist, makes it quite clear that society is of capital importance to the action: by itself, the spatial disposition of action bears out the point as the heroine moves back and forth repeatedly between the court and her anti-social retreat. Thus, for good or ill in the reader's judgment, it is still the text's society which generates convention and which prompts the Princesse to react.

Other points about which there seems to be general concensus (with remarkably little disagreement) can easily be summarized, and should

be included in a comprehensive discussion of the social milieu of the novel's action. Germane as they are to our own questions of history and narratorial perspective, these points also illuminate the general reading of a text in which the social unit serves as both catalyst and foil for the protagonist's choices. Let us examine these areas of common understanding, and look into some of their further implications.
a) Many critics express awareness that the heroine's relationship with society does nothing less than define her textual and temporal existence. It is phrased succinctly by Manfred Kusch:

> The fact that we know almost nothing about her before her appearance at court and that she dies shortly after she leaves, demonstrates, incidentally, with what absoluteness the court is postulated as *le monde*. She is born when she enters society, she dies when she withdraws from it.[11]

Seen within its parameters of the social circle—that circle which occupies the narrator's attention to the exclusion of all others—the heroine's existence assumes the aspect of a *mise en abîme*. We see her life set between the obscurity preceding her arrival at court and the oblivion of her final withdrawal; the view that we have of the heroine during this chronological cross-section shows her life clearly divided between the activity of the court setting and her retreat from that setting; finally, that retreat is itself marked by an alternation of turbulence and *repos*. Thus, the opposition activity/inactivity is recognized as a structuring device having ramifications on the social level: there, it is contact with (and activity within) society which constitutes the heroine's experience; retreat from society provides introspection concerning that experience, and not the total insulation which the Princesse ostensibly seeks. In this way, she remains a fundamentally social creature in the reader's eye, despite her numerous anti-social comments. To counter F.L. Lawrence's objection that "unless the activities of this court—ambition, galanterie, intrigue, licence—are held as a definition of life, I fail to see how the resolution of the Princesse de Clèves can be interpreted as a rejection of life, a retreat into nothingness,"[12] we need only say that these and the other activities of the court do, in fact, define life as this novel portrays it,

---

[11] Manfred Kusch, "Narrative Technique and Cognitive Modes in *La Princesse de Clèves*," *Symposium*, 30 (Winter 1976), 313. See also, for example, Serge Doubrovsky, *"La Princesse de Clèves*: une interprétation existentielle," *La Table Ronde*, 138 (June 1959), 49; also Sterling Haig, p. 133.

[12] Francis L. Lawrence, p. 20.

particularly in light of the narrator's selected vision and sense of narrative protocol.

b) The effect of this narratorial selectiveness is, as virtually all the critics agree, the depiction of a circumscribed world and an equally circumscribed social unit. With attention focused uniquely on the court society, the reader is easily persuaded that, within the parameters of the text, this is the only locus of active life.[13] We have already noted the text's limited purview of social caste; such selectiveness is not only social in nature, but spatial and temporal as well. As Kusch has stated, with reference to lexical frequency in the narrative,

> *Tout, tout le monde, partout,* and *toujours* together indicate the absoluteness and closed character of the world in which the action of the novel takes place. For *tout le monde* is court society, *partout* is the court, and *toujours* is "les dernières années du règne de Henri II."[14]

Perhaps Doubrovsky is hasty in dismissing "les besoins du récit," choosing instead to explain the circumscription about the text's world as "le symbole même de leur claustration."[15] The debate concerning two such textual functions has come to be known as the opposition between *discours* and *histoire*.[16] We can elect to say, of course, that the needs of the narrative are indeed well served by the restrictions placed on narratorial perception. It is, in fact, another means of heightening the atmosphere of crisis: if the heroine, even in retreat, were able to extricate herself totally from the closed social circle of activity, the intensity of passion and the necessity of choice would be decidedly assuaged; instead, the heroine remains *visible* (to use the term literally and figuratively) even at Coulommiers—visible to the reader and to Nemours who intrudes, physically and psychologically, upon her intended retreat several times—and she is unable to sever the ties which bind her to society until the very end of the novel, at which point she also dies. Therefore it can be argued that, in some measure, the narrator's exclusiveness of vision is dictated by the nature of the narrative. By the same token, this narrative points back to the society which it creates, and underscores the vital properties of the role it

---

[13] See Doubrovsky, pp. 37-38, who cites Antoine Adam's remarks on the very issue. See also Kusch, pp. 311-12.

[14] Kusch, p. 312.

[15] Doubrovsky, p. 38.

[16] See Jonathan Culler's chapter "Story and Discourse in the Analysis of Narrative" in *The Pursuit of Signs: Semiotics, Literature, Deconstruction* (Ithaca: Cornell University Press, 1981), pp. 169-87.

plays. And thus, the society of *La Princesse* is circumscribed in effect and by necessity: in effect, because narratorial attention is strictly delimited, ostensibly by the narrator's interests and purposes; by necessity, because the nature of the narrative requires that the heroine be encircled with no means of escape.

c) The notion of what is *visible* is capital to the text and to the society it portrays, not only in narrative strategy, but also in the thematic plan. In the narrator's speech, great emphasis is placed on the outward *éclat* and trappings of splendor, to the exclusion of commentary on the inner corruption. These priorities are mirrored in the society itself, where appearances are considered all-important without concern for the integrity of the *être* beneath.[17]

One critic dissents in recognizing the dynamics of sight in the text: M. Kusch speaks of the devaluation of visual impressions and the playing down of the physical world.[18] But to consider such "devaluation" is to ignore an important facet of the narrative, namely the undermining, few visual images which are themselves misinterpreted significantly. Perhaps the issue could be clarified by the argument that the physical world of visual signs is not devalued but capable of being misread — for crucial problems can arise due to characters' failure to understand what they see, leading us to the semiological discussion of the degree of reliability of the visible sign rather than to the idea that the physical world is deprived of meaning in the novel.

Quite to the contrary, the physical world retains its relevance.[19] First, it is the world which provides the social context, the society where the *être/paraître* opposition is constantly operative. Second, this opposition is a component of a larger textual phenomenon: the countermotif of outward signs that eventually prove to be unreliable, and which can engender flaws in the society's system of communication, taking a thematic cue from the eye of Henri II through which he is mortally wounded.[20] Finally, there is no way to minimize the

[17] Cf. Turnell, p. 39, and Vigée, p. 728.

[18] Kusch, pp. 315-16. What is confusing about this argument is that it follows compelling statistical data to the contrary, and that its reasoning seems to build a case for the importance of the visual game of appearances on the thematic level. Kusch goes on to cite passages from the novel which would assert the motif in their vocabulary (Kusch, pp. 317, 319): "les yeux," "aveugler," "des vues claires et distinctes." In this vein, consider Doubrovsky, p. 45.

[19] See Peter Brooks's remarks concerning social dynamics of the visual in this novel, chapter 2.

[20] See Singerman, p. 265, for further development of this notion.

significance of the visual token of representation and exchange, i.e. the portrait.

The society's visual orientation, evident in the stock which it places in appearances (beauty, facial expression, dress, *éclat*, and so on), is made manifest in the worth which individuals attach to portraits of persons beloved. The visual representation is raised in value to the point where it is considered an objectification of the person in question: Nemours takes the portrait of the heroine as a token of value, preferring to withdraw from company in order to contemplate it; the Princesse, for her part, spends an evening in seclusion contemplating the painting of Nemours which she has discretely procured, then she flees the presence of the person represented when she becomes aware of it. In each case, the object replaces or stands for the person beloved, occupying a place of symbolic value and high priority — and each object is a visual one, to keep the person present as more than a mental image, yet absent in the flesh. It is a *précieux* kind of idealized love.

d) The text's social plan is called a "baroque society" by F.L. Lawrence, and is seen as a sphere of perpetual motion.[21] Furthermore, the corpus of criticism on the novel tends to view this "agitation" as a part of the danger which faces the heroine, and also as a force which threatens to undermine the order of society.[22] It must be mentioned, however, that critical understanding of such a threat generally remains a moral assessment (i.e. the possible collapse of moral values), where the potential exists for the undermining of the political system as well. But let us hasten to add that political implications are carefully circumscribed, just as the society is, and that we speak of politics here as an extension of social dynamics within the court: the overall stability of the monarchy or of the nobility (as opposed, say, to their relation with the unseen bourgeoisie) is never called into question, again as a function of the "closed circle" of narratorial interest; and at any rate, the king seems to be above the socio-political intrigue which somehow has little effect on international policy while actually dominating the affairs of the circumscribed aristocracy.

e) Given this context for action, and given the parameters which the text assigns to it, we must logically ask what the nature of love is within this society. Doubrovsky rightly refers to love as "une guerre des moi," a war of egos, the idea being that the heroine especially insists that

---

[21] Lawrence, p. 16.
[22] Turnell, p. 37.

love be conducted on her terms alone.[23] These circumstances are projected over the society as a whole where ambition becomes so immeshed with passion that it is difficult to determine if the latter kindles the former, or vice-versa.

Haig's reading of the relationship between love and society sheds additional light on the subject. The implications of his commentary on the narrative "digressions" and on the "screen" characters (i.e. those who voice conscience to the heroine)[24] suggest that the social context, as it is presented, is the medium which brings about the bankruptcy of the institution of marriage. For all intents and purposes, marriage is subservient to concerns of social politics, and stands thus as a force diametrically opposed to love. And according to the evidence, virtually no character is in love with his or her spouse, from the king on down the social register. So the conclusion to be drawn is that society's formal institutions are inhospitable to those passions to which individuals are all the more sensitive. This leaves only the informal institution of *galanterie* for the conduct of affairs of the heart.

Consequently, love has only negative effects when judged by standards of the social context, and this can only be expected in a situation where it is incompatible with social institution. Undoubtedly, this is the reason why society, as Turnell sees it, tailors its definition of virtue to fit the shortcomings of human nature, thus reducing a morality of absolute standards to a uniquely social code of appearances.[25]

f) There remains the consideration of any metaphysics which would be pertinent to society. Critics (most notably Turnell, Doubrovsky, and Vigee) have generally been aware of the complete absence of God from the list of operative forces in the work; Doubrovsky in particular is attuned to the fact of a resultant metaphysical void. This is to say that the absence of God and the inertness of spirituality in the text deprive humanity of a metaphysical basis or context.[26]

It then becomes a question of how the individual or society fills that void and replaces the absent metaphysical context. The fact that neither God nor Nature provides any context within the narrative calls our attention more vividly to whatever setting there is to define meaning: the only standard by which the individual can measure life,

[23] Doubrovsky, p. 48.
[24] Haig, pp. 110-19.
[25] Turnell, pp. 38-39.
[26] Doubrovsky, p. 50.

and by which the reader can assign relative meaning, is the all-important social standard that is constantly held up to the protagonist for comparison and contrast. It is not religion, but the social norm, which Mme de Chartres uses to calibrate her ethical system; questions of metaphysics or human ontology are never present to the mind of the Princesse whose attentions are restricted to the circle of her own existence; even a crucial event like the *aveu* is judged by all who know of it as quite out of the ordinary—not for its virtue, but as it is measured by the gauge of social custom. It is indeed the social context that stands in for the missing theological (or ideological) basis for meaning, and the proof is in the way meaning is generated in the insulated locus of action. The text's society derives meaning from within its own system.

Should the issue arise on the level of narration (instead of the level of action), a most complementary explanation is offered by Kusch who holds that

> By indicating a definite time-frame, the author marks the place the period holds in the chronology of history. By filling this frame with stylized attributes, she creates a homogeneous temporal closure in which movement may exist.[27]

In other words, the narrator defines relevance by historiographic perspective, in the absence of metaphysical criteria. And of course in this novel, historiographic priorities are fixed in the social setting, since history and society are functions of one another in the text.

In semiological analysis, the social organization reveals its importance in the processes by which information is exchanged and evaluated by individuals. Society is the context for the communicative act. It is the frame in which (and often about which) communication is effected. It is ever present conceptually in characters' minds, ever ready to impose itself on their definition of priorities. When judgment, even moral judgment, is to be rendered, society's values and anticipated reactions are considered. Participating in these ways and to such a degree in the dynamics of communication, social context is the structural *system* (as the Structuralists understand the term) which circumscribes and validates the meaning of the sign in interpersonal exchanges.

---

[27] Kusch, p. 310.

VI

Of distinct promise is the study of the *visible* in the narrative as it leads us to investigate the general sign system that is operative in the court society. The semiotic ramifications of the particular conflict between visual and verbal communication are far reaching, to be sure, with significant effects in the areas of action and social structure. But this opposition finds its most important and revealing implications when the question of history is brought to the fore.

It has been made evident in our consideration of the social context for action that the society's codified sign systems prove to be, if nothing else, inconsistent. On the one hand, the farther characters stray from direct and non-referential communication (i.e. what they *see* and allow to be seen without further encoding), the more likely they are to encounter confusion, ambiguity, and misunderstanding. The language of words, especially with respect to love, can be insufficient; as we examine circuits of communication along the line of decreasing directness from the visual, through the verbal, to the indirect verbal (written) form, we note that the more the sign system is made second order and objectified, the more it tends to engender confusion and duality. The prime example of this would be the Vidame's letter. Conversely, it is through seeing that the characters are likely (though not always certain) to grasp significance: the Princesse sees her colors at the tournament and recognizes the significance, effecting the conveyance of meaning as Nemours intended; these visual objects and others (like the "canne des Indes" and the ribbons of the "mesmes couleurs qu'il avoit portées au tournoy," p. 1227) become symbols, with signifying value in their own right, by virtue of the way they are regarded. And the great "seer" throughout the novel, the one who consistently sees beyond the images which words try to create, is the Duc de Guise: at the heroine's introduction to Nemours, Guise foresees their mutual attraction (perhaps, as we are told, from the Princesse's facial reaction, p. 1127); later Guise detects her true feelings (at the lists when Nemours is injured), again by the visible reaction which she shows (p. 1168).

Nemours, for his part, overhears the entire verbal exchange of the *aveu*, but even after it all he is uncertain as to its meaning: "...son esprit s'égaroit à chercher celuy dont Mme de Clèves vouloit parler" (p. 1196). Certainty is only established by the heroine's reference to the theft of her portrait and to her witnessing the act (N.B. the code of the visual). But nothing reinforces this certainty nor delights

Nemours more than seeing the Princesse contemplating his picture and the "canne des Indes" (p. 1227). The scene revolves around the description in terms of the visual: "Voir... une personne qu'il adoroit, la voir sans qu'elle sçeust qu'il la voyoit, et la voir tout occupée de choses qui avoient du rapport à luy..." (p. 1227). The metonymy of the visible object clearly displaces the metaphor of language in the conduct of love, and to the same extent, the act of seeing provides more certainty than that of hearing: the language of most intensity and directness is the one of visible phenomena rather than the medium of words.

But at this juncture we encounter a problem concerning verbal language, for if sight and objects constitute the language of the passions, it is words which are the stuff of history. Story-telling is a concretization of language, used for almost rhetorical (i.e. predetermined) purposes, used according to conventions of narration (i.e. conventionalized), yet it meets with remarkable success: the heroine certainly gets the intended message, and history (both as stories told to the heroine, and as the interpretation and ethical value of those stories) becomes a dynamic and determinant thematic force. And what is history if not language in action, telling the story of the invisible past via narration and words?

This is indeed an issue since, as seems evident elsewhere in the text, language is thematically devalued as a vehicle of communication for the characters. In terms evaluating the reliability of verbal language, its inconsistency is pointed up in the contradiction between ineffective and effective communication. One could try to justify the paradox or manipulate the elements around to a seemingly harmonious synthesis. However, since the text offers no such unifying resolution, there is no reason to assume that the reader should either. Thus it would seem a more worthwhile endeavor to uncover further manifestations of the contradiction on other levels, if in fact there is a pattern of unresolved dissonance.

To integrate the paradoxical question of language into our reading, we should relate it to the idealism/pessimism dialectic, found by our study to be an integral part of the narrative strategy. Presently, the "language" contradiction reduces into this unresolved dialectic in the following manner: *idealistic* is the implied conclusion concerning history as a dynamic force, because that history shows the successful use of the conventionalized code and because it serves the ends of a moral system that is, by general understanding, quite positive and laudable in itself; *pessimistic* is the breakdown of verbal communication in the main — the failure of characters to speak sincerely, the imposing by polite society of trite formulae upon language, in short, the reflection of corruption in other areas of convention (namely, the institution of marriage and the supposedly intransigent social hierarchy within the aristocracy).

One definite reason why this opposition cannot be resolved into critical synthesis is that within one of the elements of polarity there occurs a framed polar opposition, drawn according to the very same parameters. The effects of history-telling are positive and promising by the standards of the accepted moral system, yet they are curiously pessimistic at the same time since history itself predicts and necessitates the novel's ending — an ending whereby earthly happiness is judged incompatible with perfection, love engenders only negative or evil consequences, and moral rigor requires anti-social retreat. History thus mirrors within itself the central ambiguity.

Given this dimension of the idealism/pessimism dialectic, it seems that synthesis cannot be achieved since at least one of the polar elements is unstable. Consequently, the opposition relative to the sign system of language remains a paradox on the textual level of action. But this should come as no surprise since the novel's action turns on the same axis: the heroine's idealistic effort to reconcile her ethics with society is frustrated at every turn, leading one to draw decidedly pessimistic inferences.

Earlier we saw a reflection of the opposition in narrative voice. There it afforded no resolution either, so we see a pattern developing. The text is intent on countering idealism with pessimism, but it will not resolve the contradiction in favor of one or the other. Nor will it draw the two poles into a middle ground of compromise. This is where the matter must remain if the novel is to contract, not to resolve this issue, but to relate the story of a princess who cannot realize the portents of happiness while fulfilling her own promises.

Social context is crucial to this notion and to the novel as a whole, since the unresolved oppositions are played out within the bounds of the closed circle of society. This may be deduced even by a process of elimination because, as Doubrovsky notes, God and the cosmos (including the natural world) simply do not enter into the issue as any sort of potential factors.[28] Rather, it is society's customs and codes which define the rules of the game where other rules are lacking.

---

[28] Doubrovsky, p. 50.

4. Catalysts of Action: Social Dynamics

I

Is society portrayed as it is in *La Princesse de Clèves* because of pre-defined narratorial intentions and priorities, or on the contrary, is the narrator's historical focus attracted to this society because of something inherently fascinating that it embodies? In other words, is the historian's particular interest in social dynamics a cause or an effect, an active or a reactive choice? To debate the issue is to become embroiled in a question like the one which asks if it is the chicken or the egg that first appeared. However, in considering this novel in its entirety, one senses that a productive course is to assess history and society as textual functions of one another, thoroughly interwoven as structural threads.

In a very concrete way, the phenomena of society and history are interdependent for their existence both within the text's world and in the reader's eye. It is even possible to view the novel itself as a product of the cooperation or relationship between society and history, so dynamic and pervasive are these two forces in the narrative. To consider only the broadest aspect of the novel's composition, these two provide both the material for narration as well as its frame and pretext. But the relationship between them is a symbiotic one.[1]

---

[1] Peter Brooks states that "Mme de Lafayette unquestionably profits... in general from the new attention to history, but her primary interest is in how the individual's actions are determined by his consciousness of society" (*The Novel of Worldliness* [Princeton: Princeton University Press, 1969], p. 69). I would take one more step

In the first place, historical information which is conveyed in the text does not concern wars or economics, but society. Social dynamics furnish the pretext for the secondary narratives (as in the case of the Princesse who asks for information concerning her possible "rival" for Nemours, and who wishes to be enlightened about Mme de Tournon, a character with whom the heroine is only familiar on a social level). The secondary narratives are filled with family histories, stories of marriages, love affairs, and social factions, lending the aspect of a social register to the telling of history on the level of action. The main narrator, for his part, is telling the story of a society, reflecting and expanding the effort of the secondary narrators to relate stories of famous women and of society in general. We need not elaborate on previous remarks concerning the main narrator's interest in things social; suffice it to say that the narrator-historian finds his material in the internal workings of the court society of the sixteenth century.

In addition to this, we know that history is not merely a presentational technique, but even a thematic force. With this in mind, we can see that what occurs in the novel's society is a function of the past, that is to say, a function of history or of historical consciousness. The prolepsis of the characters' historical narratives, the role of history-telling as a vehicle for stories of fate, the role of history itself as fate as it intercedes to direct the present time of action, all point to the fact that society is decidedly beholden to history and to the historical model. Mme de Chartres offers history to her daughter as a model of interpretation for reading signs of the turbulent social context of the "present"; indeed the entire society is organized and defined according to what has gone before. The long-standing rivalry between the queen and Diane de Poitiers, which the main narrator offers at the outset under the general rubric of historical background, is responsible for the structure of "cabales" at court. And the role of Diane herself is best explained by her own history which dates from the reign of François Ier.

Thus we recognize the prime importance of the relationship between history and society, the fact that they are mutually supportive and fulfilling for characters, narrator, and reader alike (or more accurately, on the levels of action, narration, and reader response). Each defines the other, for history within the novel is the story of society,

to argue that society is, in the novel, a function of history, and that society's dynamics are the very substance of the novel's internal historiography (i.e. the text's narrative plan).

and social developments (even when considered as the aggregate of individuals' fortunes) are preordained and prefigured by history. This is not to imply by any means that the novel should be read as an elaborate gossip column. Such a reading might contribute to the understanding of other novels, but not *La Princesse*, if only by virtue of the psychology of the individual in the social context. In narrative terms, the fixing of point of view in indirect style does not here have the effect of upstaging society in order to direct attention to the individual (as is the case with *Madame Bovary*, for example); instead, *La Princesse* focuses on (or adopts the focus of) the individual, but always within the tension of the social frame of reference.

The evidence indicates that society and history are bound to each other logically, thematically, and in terms of still other textual functions. History's dependence on society is immediately perceptible, as history is in this case the verbal reconstruction of a social context and of an individual life within that context. For the other part, society's dependence on history is less obvious, but no less significant or influential. It has to do first with the structure of the court society being inherited from the past; second, there is the use of historical narrative in society as a token of exchange; one might even consider third the didactic and moralizing role which history plays with respect to the protagonist. But society's reliance on history in the structure of the novel extends even further, into the development of what we may term a pattern of social "affinities."

We may begin investigating these affinities by asking what the bonds are which draw characters to one another, and create interpersonal relationships in this setting. The bond which comes to mind first is that of *love*. It is one to which virtually all characters at court, from the king downward, are sensitive. But it is curious to note that relationships inspired by the passions never seem to coincide with the relationships defined by matrimony: the only characters reported to be in love with their spouses are the king's sister and M. de Clèves; in neither case is there any mention that this love is returned.

The second kind of interpersonal bond is *political*. The reader is soon made aware of the existence of political factions at the court: "La cour estoit partagée entre MM. de Guise et le Connestable, qui estoit soutenu des princes du sang" (p. 1110). And only a few pages later, it is made explicit that politics and love are intertwined: "Il y avoit tant d'intérests et tant de cabales différentes, et les dames y avoient tant de part que l'Amour estoit toujours meslé aux affaires et les affaires à l'Amour" (p. 1117). Politics and political factions compose an integral part of the overall social backdrop against which the action of the novel is played. Likewise it is politics which defines the status of certain important court figures at every moment, as is the case with the Connestable and the Guise brothers. But as for the nature of political bonding, factions are presented to the reader as a *fait accompli*, immutable, and dating back for a considerable time in the society's past.

Other bonds include those of *blood* and *friendship*. These seem evident in themselves, yet it is most often difficult to consider them apart from the political bonds mentioned above. The blood bond of the Guise brothers, for example, is almost marginal to their collective function as a political force, as far as the novel's view can see. In the same way, mention is often made throughout the text of the blood relationship between the heroine and the Vidame, but in terms of the characters' political standing at court: for example, the Cardinal opposes a marriage between his brother and the heroine because of the family tie between her and the Vidame whom he hates (p. 1118).

As concerns sheer effectiveness, friendship appears to be of less consequence than politics: consider the fact that Nemours's friendship with Clèves does not impede him in the least from pursuing a love relationship with his friend's wife (or from looking forward to his friend's death, for that matter, p. 1234); and compare this ineffectual "friendship" with the considerable political influence which the Cardinal de Lorraine exercises on the mind of the queen. The society is shown to be a highly politicized one, and the bonds of blood and friendship do not mitigate the harshness of this situation.

The remaining sort of bond between characters is *institutional*, i.e. predicated on institutions of social nature, of which the principal one is marriage. As implied by all that has gone before, these may properly be viewed as socio-political bonds. Furthermore, they are preordained, since one's marriage is arranged by elders according to criteria quite apart from love, and since social condition is an inherited trait.

Let us note, in passing, the absence of ideological bonds, as the issue of ideology is simply inert in the society. Also, economic bonds as such are almost non-existent, except inasmuch as one's finances become a factor in the organization of a marriage contract.

What we notice most graphically in the array of interpersonal associations which the novel calls into play is their generally contingent nature. With the exception of the least effective and binding of the lot (friendship), all of them are dependent upon sets of pre-existing conditions and circumstances. In the cases of institutional, blood, and political bonds, there is a historical kind of motivation: the interpersonal bond is necessarily a function of what has been inherited or previously decreed. But one may ask: what of love relationships? In what measure can they be judged contingent upon external forces or prior circumstances?

In the first place, the novel gives us a highly detailed case in the central action for study. It happens that the first meeting of the Princesse and Nemours is a chance occurrence — it is certain that their paths will eventually cross, given the nature of the social circle, but it is by chance that their first meeting has, as M. de Guise puts it, "quelque chose de galant et d'extraordinaire" (p. 1127). Chance is a form of fate, and we have occasion to link the phenomenon of fate to the notion of history, the lone metaphysical (hence external) force operative in the action. But while fate itself is at issue, the reference to the Chevalier de Guise is most appropriate as he is the *only* character who recognizes the central love relationship from the very beginning — and even at this point, he sees the hand of fate, in that, to his mind, "...la fortune destinoit M. de Nemours à estre amoureux de Mme de Clèves" (p. 1127).[2]

But as we have seen, there is that other side to fate, the side which concerns history. It is not the power of the present to determine the future, but the complementary situation in which the present derives its meaning from the past. This dynamic of history produces the conditions whereby it is "natural," or seemingly so, for certain things to occur — things which seem at first glance to be mere chance, such as for Nemours to fall in love with Mme de Clèves. The situation, having evolved out of the past, is now favorable for these occurrences, and this is based not on the prior dictum of some absent Racinian deity, but instead on affinities of long standing that are inherited in the present. "Chance" thus is less a matter of happenstance than it appears.

It is certainly evident that the more significant interpersonal bonds, with the exception of blood and possibly love, are born of ulterior

[2] At other points, observations are attributed to Guise which reinforce his "clairvoyant" role: see pages 1134 and 1168 of the novel. He understands latent meanings, and does so before Mme de Chartres or even the heroine herself.

motives. As the question of motivation is not pertinent to blood relationships, one would ask at this point what it is that draws characters to each other romantically. Again, the novel offers only one substantial relationship of mutual attraction: examples of unrequited love abound, as do cases of unenduring mutual love, but the detail of the central love story is as unique as the love which it depicts. For other characters, the reader is left to surmise the origins and nature of attraction; the narrator, in his often quoted description of the "cabales" at court (p. 1117), seems to indicate that interests generally have their place in love as well. The boundary between politics and *galanterie* is obscured by these remarks, but one can entertain little doubt that the passions count for much in love.

By no means is love here the totally positive and constructive force which the pastoral tradition makes of it (in the abstract). It is obvious in all we have seen that love is forever an earthly relationship between mortals who are capable of mistakes. What is more, we have noted how it is actually out of harmony with the text's accepted positive codes: time and again (as with the heroine), it fails to coincide with social/institutional bonds; as a function of the passions, love is in effect a negative force which works against the implicit ethical code and which produces cumbersome consequences. But even if one were to argue for its moral worth in the text, there is no way to deny the fact that fate is set against it. The same force of fate which induces love condemns it to failure. These points alone, concerning the status of love in the scheme of the novel, should suffice to alert the reader to the work's pessimistic coloration.

However, the matter at hand is the role of fate in the origins of love. The story of the Princesse and Nemours shows these origins to be not the accidental event of pastoral usage, but instead, carefully and subtly prepared by forces other than those of the parties involved. Affinities antecede the beginning of the direct relationship, favoring it and minimizing resistance to it. In other words, conditions are previously readied, in several areas, to ensure that attraction will be mutual and that its occurrence will seem a logical consequence. Of course, it is also something of a primrose path, given the pessimism which enshrouds the presentation of the passions; likewise, it is in keeping with the unresolved tension between idealism and pessimism that fate may both necessitate and condemn the love relationship. But above all, fate loses the mysterious aura of a force of coincidence, and is seen as a more calculating force than one may at first suspect. What appear to be accidents with great import turn out to be no accidents at all, but rather, events which find plausible motivation in the "affinities" that the narrative prepares for them.

The romantic affinities of which we speak mark a convergence of factors which are components of fate, as fate is set forth in this novel. In the first place, there are the forces of Nature and heredity, which have dealt quite complementary characteristics to Nemours and to the Princesse. Both are described by the narrator as clearly superior in comparison with others in terms of physical attribute: perfection in beauty and physical aspect evidently attracts its like. Each of the characters embodies the most attractive traits of his or her sex, such as beauty, grace, good taste in appearance, and so on. This kind of ideal matching pertains also to the intellectual plane. Each shows a mental awareness of the other, able to sense even the physical presence or the psychological force of the other.

At this point, it is clear that "Nature" takes an active hand as a decisive metaphysical force. But Nature is spoken of here as an extension of fate, rather than as the cosmos: the notions of "the world in which we are born and die" or *la condition humaine* are philosophical considerations which are not pertinent to the novel's thematics or to its psychology of character, for the novel's universe is the court, and its depiction of the human condition has more to do with society than with humanity's ontology. Thus Nature, instead of assuming the role of imposing strict conditions on existence, is the absent force that provides the basic situation in which the characters subsequently interact. Nature is subsumed by fate, but as such it is less a physical than metaphysical factor. The issue of fate, then, comes down to a capital question of determination: is the society (or the individual within it) able to effect or even aspire to self-determination, or is determination imposed by pressures from without? The tension between these two conceptual models will be discussed later in this chapter.

Heredity, too, is not without significance in this circumscribed world where perfection seemingly seeks its own kind. Nemours and the Princesse are of more or less equal social rank and comparable fortune (to infer from sparse hints concerning the subject). Each looks to the other as the corresponding apex of some evolutionary process. And in a context where social rank, valor, and illustriousness are all defined in familial terms (not to mention the customary codes and values of the classical period concerning birth), it is to be expected that the discussion of "perfection" not stray far at any point from the topic of heredity.

We have detected channels of affinity in love and in heredity; both, in some way, have roots in the past. The remaining sort of affinity is of specifically historical nature, having to do with families and factions. In this area, friendships (while not of vital concern to the action itself) and socio-political affiliations provide lines of communication or even associations which run parallel to the eventual bonds of sentiment. The case in point is the situation of the Chartres family which finds itself *de facto* in the party of the queen (and hence in disfavor of Diane de Poitiers), due to the politics of the Vidame (p. 1116). Nemours himself seems to avoid being restricted to a particular faction by virtue of his universal magnetism, but one does learn that he is the "amy intime" of the Vidame (p. 1134) who shows "une grande amitié" for the heroine (p. 1116). Bonds of family and friendship, already in place, furnish a channel in which a love relationship may find its course. At any rate, the role of the Vidame as linchpin proves to be anything but gratuitous, as he plays the intermediary at several subsequent points.

Where the notion of historical affinity is even more revealing is in the relationship between the heroine and the husband-to-be. Here affinity is conspicuous by its absence. In fact, the lack of affinity between the situations of the principals is indicative of an insurmountable barrier to love. The family of the Prince de Clèves, we are told, has "d'étroites liaisons" with Diane de Poitiers (p. 1117); the narrator goes on immediately to state that Diane "estoit ennemie du Vidame," and that this condition alone provided a familial (i.e. factional) impediment to a marriage of the Prince and the heroine. For, as we have noted, the Chartres family is aligned with the queen. There is no doubt that politics are a major consideration in the establishment of what we have termed institutional bonds:

> [Mme de Chartres] n'avoit pas mis en doute que M. de Nevers ne regardast le mariage de sa fille comme un avantage pour son fils; elle fut bien estonnée que la maison de Clèves et celle de Guise craignissent son alliance, au lieu de la souhaiter. (p. 1119)

But can it be a coincidence that the heroine's affections go not to Clèves or Guise (with whom her family has no pre-existing affinity), but to Nemours?

Granted, in introducing the notion of affinities, we appear to be calling on the uncertain tenet of organic unity in a literary text, the tenet which we have repeatedly called into question with regard to the anomalies of *La Princesse*. Hence, let us distinguish between generic and specific treatment of the issue of "affinities." In *La Princesse de Clèves* in particular, we are dealing with a textual structure in which history is proleptic and determinant, an arm of fate. We have gone to lengths to show critical precedent for this idea and to elaborate on it. We are thus appealing not to a debatable principle of literary theory, but rather to a structuring device in a particular work.

As concerns the other areas of affinity, then, the point is further borne out. Alain Niderst has pointed out the disparity of narrative space offered to the portraiture of M. de Clèves and Nemours (three lines to twenty-six respectively, by Niderst's count).[3] He goes on to assert that, whereas Clèves exists in the shadow of his father as a second son, Nemours enjoys an independence and a maturity as yet unknown to his rival.[4] The social situations of these two are qualitatively different: while the one is entertaining the possibility of marriage to the queen of England, the other is second in his family and still under the tutelage of his father as the action begins. Thus, heredity leaves them in unequal positions, with Nemours having the far greater affinity with the outstanding, "perfect" heroine.

The same is true with respect to natural endowment. Clèves, despite the narrator's complimentary terms of "parfaitement bien fait" (which he shares with his brothers), "digne," and "brave et magnifique," still cuts a pale figure next to Nemours, whose description abounds in superlatives. Which of the two is more likely at the outset to win the affections of the superlative Mlle de Chartres? The obviousness of the answer to this question is precisely the point that we wish to make concerning affinities and their tacit effectiveness prior to the action.

II

These affinities act as unseen forces which point the way for action, indicating the potential of dynamism in an initially static situation. Such a situation typifies the opening of a conventional narrative that does not begin *in medias ras*. Far from joining an action already in progress, *La Princesse* takes care first to trace the circle in which events will transpire, then to introduce the actors; during the course of this

---

[3] Alain Niderst, *'La Princesse de Clèves': le roman paradoxal* (Paris: Larousse, 1973), p. 41.
[4] Niderst, p. 41.

initial presentation, the structure of affinities begins to take shape, later to be reinforced. Chronologically, then, the affinities are really a part of the process of the circumscription of action in that they stand apart from the events themselves, but offering both logical incentive and a particular channel for action.

We have entered the domain of motivation, where the structure of affinities is an inherited facet of the scene which is set prior to the unfolding of action. The term "structure" is not used loosely: at this point we may verbalize an opposition that displaces further the notion of harmony in this novel. Within the overall phenomenon of history, we perceive a reflection of one of the novel's more central and overt conflicts. On the one hand, it has seemed evident in all our conclusions concerning history that it is a moral force, determinant in the triumph of duty over passion. But on the other hand, history is responsible for a contrary set of affinities, whereby characters find themselves destined to be attracted to the "wrong" persons. In other words, the action's central conflict is preordained in the dynamic of history which antecedes action as its thematic backdrop and its temporal predecessor.

History, by its own moral criteria, is thus responsible at the same time for right and wrong—a pessimistic conclusion drawn from a supposedly ideal phenomenon, and one with which we are by now familiar. As before, we find that the novel affords no tidy resolution of the conflict on that metaphysical level of history. Indeed, the struggle is an implicit one, as a more overt confrontation would be too pointed an issue to remain in logical suspense. So, to the extent that history tacitly crosses its purposes, human nature is shown to do the same in more evident fashion. It is then a simple matter for the text to shift the venue of the central conflict to the level of action—a love story in which, as centuries of criticism have indicated, resolution is no less ambiguous than it is fleeting on the level of history. In that action, a woman sets a goal of moral perfection for herself and then proceeds to compromise her ideal; she seeks *repos* in a turbulent world; she longs for an impossible happiness. The list of self-contradictions goes on, reflecting history's own inner paradox.

The question of motivation then comes to the fore: what, in the present time of action, plays the motivational role parallel to that of the historical affinities? What is at the source of the direction taken in the protagonist's crucial decisions? The effort to answer these questions has occupied many critics recently. Assessments of the source of moral obligation in the novel gravitate around two poles: the recognition of religious influence in moral choice, and the denial of such influence in favor of a humanistic definition of morality. Critics espousing the latter view are decidedly in the majority, and we need not reiterate the arguments in favor of this position. Where H.K. Kaps and F.L. Lawrence may cite the single reference to the "maison religieuse" and the Christian world view of seventeenth-century France,[5] it nevertheless seems more fitting to attribute a principal thematic of morality in this novel to a more principal source, that is to say, a dynamic force which stands behind the operative moral code and which is at least as visible and vital as that code. Ethical motivation arises from a force that is easily confused with a Christian one. But it is only an inference that the protagonist's choices are of religious origin, while it is earthly and social values which make up the expressed influential factors in the shaping of choice. If a coincidence with Christian ends is seen, it must be understood as a contextual — rather than textual — phenomenon. For this reason, it is more consistent to associate metaphysical decisions with the novel's only manifestation of metaphysical influence, one which emanates from the social level (instead of the divine), namely history.

Critical definitions of anthropocentric moral premises cover the spectrum from *orgueil* and narcissism,[6] through a neutral set of bourgeois values,[7] to an idealistic kind of humanism consisting of some balance between virtue (more or less for its own sake) and a quest for *repos*.[8] All of these appraisals are correct, as there is evidence in the text to support each one. The fact that all of these bases coexist points to the complexity of moral obligation, but most of them have to do with the dynamic interplay between the individual psyche and the social milieu.

It is, of course, no new revelation to assert that the development of a moral code is of primary thematic importance in *La Princesse*. What does deserve emphasis, however, is the fact that the locus of central conflict in the quest is found in the relationship between the individual and her society. There the issue is precisely the ill-fatedness of the effort to reconcile the ideal with the realities of life in society,

---

[5] Cf. Helen K. Kaps, pp. 24-26 and Francis L. Lawrence, p. 21.
[6] Cf. Serge Doubrovsky, pp. 37-39 and Claude Vigée.
[7] Cf. Martin Turnell, and Vigée, p. 728, in some measure.
[8] Cf. Simone Fraisse, p. 565, and William O. Goode, p. 401; see also Niderst, *'La Princesse de Clèves': le roman paradoxal*, pp. 111-12.

in view of the limitations of the human condition which beset both the society and the individual. Given this, along with the narrator's dual preoccupation with the heroine's moral quest and social context, the principal lines of opposition are drawn between "reality" and a moral ideal, where the former remains unalterable, and the latter, an abstraction.

The crucial point is that, despite this degree of abstraction, and despite even the metaphysical properties of history in the narrative, the purview of action and narrative vision does not go beyond *society*. Social context, circumscribed as it is, constitutes the sphere of opposition. Hence the narrator chooses to examine the workings of society at its best (an individual's effort to live the social code of *éclat* to the letter) and at its worst (deception, adultery, hypocrisy, and the rest). With the interaction of morality and social structure, it is logical that the narrator's attention does not stray from the visible social plane: the individual's moral crisis involves society, and morality itself is always expressed in social (rather than spiritual) terms. Justification of so sweeping a statement does not rest solely on the text's silence on matters of religion; instead, the practice and preaching of ethics find an actual basis in the system of social conventions which may be referred to as "contract law."

III

It is the very absence of a transcendental, or theocentric, kind of morality which calls for a definition of the basis of social order. The forces of disorder are considerable in light of the religious vacuum, the atmosphere of intrigue, and the intransigence of the noble ego. If this world is not to be reeling in chaos, some ethical system must be in force to serve as a legal foundation and structuring principle for social order; otherwise, the social unit could not function, and certainly it would be impossible to maintain even the appearances of order, harmony, and glory which count for so much in the narrative as we read it. But there is such an operative ordering principle, and it is depicted in social terms since it builds on interpersonal relationships. And thus it is a law which does not reach beyond the social plane for justification, comprising instead a series of contracts into which humans enter for the sake of filling human needs.

Vital to the notion of *contract* is the fact that it is a human phenomenon, of human making. The issue of freedom of choice is complicated by such factors as historical predetermination and historical affinity, but it is true at the same time that characters at least judge themselves to be in a position to renegotiate or reinterpret their commitments. Nemours, for example, attempts to effect just such a change in the Princesse's understanding of her contractual obligation to her husband. When Nemours and the heroine converse for the last time in the novel, Nemours is pleading his case as a lawyer would, and he does so in somewhat legal phrasing, challenging the heroine's interpretation of the "law," and submitting another plausible construct to replace it:

> ...il n'y a plus de devoir qui vous lie,... je vous dirois mesme qu'il dépend de vous de faire en sorte que vostre devoir vous oblige un jour à conserver les sentiments que vous avez pour moi. (p. 1245)
>
> ...quel fantôme de devoir opposez-vous à mon bonheur? (p. 1245)
>
> Vous l'avez fait par une vertu austère, qui n'a presque point d'exemple; mais cette vertu ne s'oppose plus à vos sentimens et j'espère que vous les suivrez malgré vous. (p. 1248)
>
> ...vous seule vous imposez une loy que la vertu et la raison ne vous sçauroient imposer. (p. 1249)

The conversation is a debate, and Nemours' tone is clearly rhetorical: what he is trying to do is to persuade Mme de Clèves to void a previous contract in favor of a new, more compelling one. Obviously, the key word during this, the longest conversation reported between the Princesse and Nemours, is *devoir*. It occurs an extraordinary number of times, not only in the sense of "duty," but also in the sense of what is owed by one character to another as a matter of mutual and informed consent. To this sort of commitment characters remain faithful, out of a sense of honor, out of recognition of the binding nature of an agreement.

Contracts, being interpersonal understandings, are social in nature. As such they help to define the relationship between the individual and society. They are diverse in kind as the novel sets them forth: they may be political (as in the king's negotiations with Spain), they may be emotional (like the *liaison* between the Vidame de Chartres and the queen), or institutional (as with marriage in the way that the characters view it), or they may even be narrative pacts (those agreements which bring about the telling of intercalated stories). In short, they follow the principal lines of interpersonal bonds as discussed above. But in all cases, the bonds of contract serve to join the parties together, contributing to the formation of a dynamic and closed social unit. Characters, even in seclusion or retreat, do not long remain apart from the society which alone offers them stimulation and *élan*. They, like the perspective of the narrator, do not wander far from the society which, for better or worse, creates their identity and surrounds their lives.

If we agree, as most critics concur, that the protagonist's moral system is a human phenomenon, a "morale laïque," then it is a short and logical step to associate it with the notion of contract law. Contractual agreement is the glue which binds the constituent parts of the novel's social institutions, the only bond, that is, aside from characters' membership in the noble class which is a function of birth. It is mutual consent upon which the processes of social unity are predicated—the agreement of the players to abide by the rules of the game, whether the game be love, socializing, storytelling, or in the heroine's case, duty. Playing by the rules perpetuates the game and keeps it (as well as the novel) interesting. But it is to be stressed that the heroine's actions and choices constitute a kind of *social* game where she and other humans agree on its rules and conduct.

As concerns the Princesse, the prime basis is that society is in the role of spectator: for her, it is a question of what society is not to see. In the absence of spiritual considerations, events fall into the domain of social proceedings where social appearances are all-important, and where one withdraws from the game only by withdrawing from society. This is precisely what the heroine does, but only after a considerable effort at playing in a test of wills with Nemours. The point is that the overriding concern for her, the only concern, is a social one: her conduct in the action, and her final retreat from society, are determined by her sense of fidelity to contractual commitments. In this respect we see the heroine to be a social creature, not the total recluse which criticism often makes of her. When she retreats into solitude, she does so not out of an anti-social instinct, but rather as a result of contracts which she chooses to honor.

Thus the heroine's mundane morality is a socially inspired phenomenon, backed by human convention. Her marriage is a social, or rather, a socio-political liaison, governed by the laws of honor which, in her eyes, protect any binding contract. Contract it is, and much more legal than sentimental, for it is premised on concerns for prestige and appearances—social concerns like those which are pre-eminent for Mme de Chartres in her choice of a son-in-law. When the Princesse is finally in a position to effect a choice after her husband's death, she is still psychologically encumbered by the contract of social morality which she accepted from the hands of her mother.

The reader is told early on that Mme de Chartres is "extrêmement glorieuse" (p. 1114), and her concern for social appearances is evident as she endeavors to find a suitable match for her daughter. In spite of her idealization of love in marriage, the mother demonstrates values which are very much of this world. In fact, the disparity is so great that there arises a considerable contradiction in this regard. On the one hand, she teaches her daughter that a woman's happiness is "d'aimer son mary et d'en estre aimée" (p. 1113). Yet, in spite of the fact that the young girl feels "aucune inclination" for the person of M. de Clèves (p. 1122) and tells her mother so, Mme de Chartres is anxious to marry her daughter to "un mary qu'elle ne pust aimer..." (p. 1122) Depriving the heroic moral system of its basis in human inclination, this self-contradiction sheds pessimistic light on the ideal, portraying it as unattainable, and shows that the source of the moral code is in the society rather than in the psyche of the individual.

In the absence of an emotional commitment, the heroine enters into the contract of marriage as into a social bond based on social obligations. She does not love her husband, but is first made aware by someone else (fittingly, by her mother) of "ce qu'elle devoit à l'inclination qu'il luy avoit temoignée... dans un temps ou personne n'osoit plus penser à elle" (p. 1124). The verb *devoir*, with social implications, resounds early and turns into a leitmotif for the heroine's marriage relationship by dint of repetition. It is subsequently understood that, in exchange for a suitable marriage situation, the Princesse will owe her husband fidelity and allegiance. Before and after the wedding, the man regrets the lack of ardor in her feelings for him, but she is committed only to the letter of the contract. Throughout the marriage, the Princesse is clearly living out the terms of such an agreement. Only once does she come close to investing more of herself, as she shows "plus d'amitié et plus de tendresse qu'elle n'avoit encore fait;" (p. 1142, upon the death of her mother), but it is crucial to note that these remarks are preceded immediately by an expression of her desire more than ever "de ne manquer à rien de ce qu'elle luy devoit." The verbe *devoir* in its contractual sense appears again to qualify the marital relationship.

So systematically is the heroine's marriage typified by terms of duty that an established pattern is evident in a few citations from among the many possible. Mme de Chartres says:

Songez ce que vous devez à votre mari; songez ce que vous devez à vous-mesme,... (p. 1141).

The heroine herself states:

...je suivray les règles austères que mon devoir m'impose. (p. 1245)

And again,

Veux-je manquer à M. de Clèves? Veux-je me manquer à moy-mesme? (p. 1191)

The heroine herself couches her remarks habitually in this legalistic code which is quite symptomatic of her general attitude toward marriage. Fidelity and some vague "estime" for M. de Clèves are recognized as her sole explicit obligations under the agreement to which she will adhere legalistically, if not in spirit. But then, "spirit" does not functionally matter for two reasons: first, the contract, being a social agreement, requires only social (that is, outward) compliance; and second, even though the psychological conflict pursuant to the contract is one of duty versus love, the world view is different from, say, classical tragedy since spiritual factors are inert in the novel.

Given the protagonist's lack of understanding and experience at the opening of the novel, it is obvious that her concept of marriage and marital obligation is acquired as the action unfolds. Where the beliefs originate and how the heroine assumes them are no great mysteries since they constitute a pre-existing model, transmitted by mother and husband, and accepted in its entirety. The model rests on the complementary notions of agreement and exchange which make of marriage (in theory and in practice) an actual contract. The authority of the contract is necessarily one of convention, as supernatural explanations do not apply and the natural order seems never to support the marriage relationship with mutual, personal attraction. The Princesse continually asserts in word and thought that her husband is most worthy of her love and fidelity—but by what standard? This question is never explicitly answered, but clearly the husband's claims are not based on the same natural order which renders Nemours so superior to Clèves and so fitting a match for the heroine. The conventional nature of the contract thus defines it as a social (and arbitrary) agreement, one to which each of the responsible parties consents before the fact, but also one which represents for the Princesse a rational, as opposed to sentimental, bond.

It is the rational world which is codified and filled with signifying formalities. If half of the heroine's textual life is spent in the silence of solitude, the other, more challenging half is spent in this domain of the verbal, the arena of society, vows, and contracts. This is not the locus of fortuitous events, private passions, or tacit communication; rather it is that of institutionalized meanings and rigid custom, both inherited from the past. One of the primary motivating forces in this world is certainly duty, and it is conceptualized by the heroine as absolute insofar as contractual obligations are concerned—hence her resolve in the *dénouement* of action.

However, her character is not entirely rational, and thus her recognition of this absoluteness is not totally constant. Sensitive as she is to the attractiveness of violating the constraints of duty, she may puzzle the reader who is seeking to identify the positive moral code.[9] Readers may prefer to assess her deeds in light of her final stand, but the fact is that, despite her heated denials of complicity in a love affair (e.g. p. 1196), few could deny that she wavers in thought as well as in deed. Her breach of contract is what constitutes her guilt, the guilt which paradoxically will cause her to observe the contract most rigorously when it is no longer binding. But when she states to her questioning husband: "...je n'ay jamais fait d'action dont je n'eusse souhaité que vous eussiez esté témoin" (p. 1235), can the reader not challenge the assertion to some degree? This debate may even extend to the heroine's "wish," but certainly regards her "actions" of which the reader, unlike the husband, is aware. But even the husband has been witness to the striking of another, tacit contract—this one, between the Princesse and Nemours—which stands in direct opposition to the heroine's marriage. It takes the form of a pattern of behavior whereby the heroine, despite her claims to the contrary, communicates non-verbal signs of favor to Nemours who, we are repeatedly told, interprets them as such; she in turn receives his visual and encoded verbal expressions of love. As the Princesse refuses to attend the Mareschal's ball, hears willingly Nemours's amorous intent concerning the telling of his fortune, watches the theft of her portrait, an overtone of complicity is heard in disharmony with her supposedly consistent sense of duty. Then, when the opposition of love and duty is fully set out and the heroine finds herself in "grande extrémité," three forces converge on her in immediate succession to predestine the famous *aveu* and the

[9] The narrator, as noted above, is reluctant to offer explicit judgment, and this includes an overt identification of what would be "proper" for the heroine to do.

eventual outcome of the action: 1) "...ce que Mme de Chartres luy avoit dit an mourant..." that is, a lesson in contractual obligation; 2) "Ce que M. de Clèves luy avoit dit sur la sincérité,..." or historical *récit;* and 3) "...il luy sembla qu'elle... devoit avouer..." again, the verb *devoir* serving as leitmotif for her understanding of marital fidelity (pp. 1165-66).

In the end she seems to recognize her failure to abide by the strictest terms of her first and more binding contract with M. de Clèves. For this reason she imposes an earthly sentence on herself which entails the withdrawal from society and the refusal of happiness. The legalistic stand which she takes when the contract is no longer in effect is indicative of the importance of the overall notion of "contract" and the system in which contracts function. The system is a codified component of a larger and more complex social network of codes governing interpersonal, political and institutional bonds. The legal element of the network is comprised of the contract system, in the absence of any other functional (or necessary) legal code for the society.

That the system of contracts is recognized and operative is a matter of great impact on the plot since the heroine's moral ideal is a morality by contract. The narrator, for example, may pose as a moralist only for the ironic purpose of showing the heroic code to be, as the text's last word states, "inimitable." But the heroine herself is undeniably some sort of serious moralist by her own agreement, preoccupied with the ethical system that she does not even always observe. One may find fault with her eventual choice of code, or recognize it as a set of bourgeois values; one may ascribe her final decision to the self-consciousness of fiction, calling it "overtly non-human" instead of "superhuman." Still, she is the moralist, but her morality is decidedly mundane.

This represents a nuance for morality in the literature of the 1670s. Regardless of any Jansenist leanings attributed to Mme de Lafayette,[10] this is a text whose moral crisis is without supernatural dimension. The establishment of the positive moral code is thematically central, yet its values are left up to the individual will and the individual's environment, that is, society. This leaves the novel's thematic axis somewhere between the *moralistes* and the *mondains*.

The differences with Racinian morality are obvious, but functionally speaking, there is a similarly inexorable, predetermined moral code

---

[10] See Alain Niderst, *'La Princesse de Clèves' de Mme de Lafayette* (Paris: Nizet, 1977), pp. 154-61.

in effect in the novel. The point is that, even if it is a model which the protagonist inherits, it is not one of divine origin, but rather of human making. It is set by what the Princesse views as history: the memory of her mother, the historical moralizing tales which are narrated to her, and of course her own marriage contract, itself established largely by the heroine's mother.

At this point, one may well ask: what is the difference if the same moral code derives from either a divine or historical source? The difference is that a human code admits of human participation and choice, of on-going definition and interpretation: and this is precisely what occurs in the novel. In a manner of speaking, the story of the heroine's moral formation is the novel—not a Racinian tragedy which we read, but a novel.

It is *choice* which gives rise to the notion of contract as regards morality. From this perspective, the Princesse is seen to accept the code which is preached by her mother, based albeit on the value of social appearances and the call to rise above the shortcomings of other women. Her only other choice is whether she will honor that agreement, and that is where the moral implications cease, for the law which stands behind her contractual commitments is a law of human and worldly proportion.

IV

Our investigation of the text's action has led us to consider as primary catalysts the systems of bonds, affinities, and contracts, all of them tributaries of the confluent forces of history and social dynamics. Several conclusions can be drawn upon our observations.

First, the cohesion of the text's social fabric is provided by those bonds, affinities, and contracts (which contracts may be considered as outward, more formalized bonds predicated on the mutual consent of the parties). Here the novel differs from classical tragic vision where a society's unity, for as much as it matters, is largely a function of its theology. At any rate, as we narrow our attention to the system of contractual interpersonal ties, we notice that there is, in the novel's principal action, a disparity between the ways in which the individual and the society regard the contract: in this opposition, both the nature and the duration of contractual obligation are in question.

Secondly, we note that the heroine herself is not entirely of one mind on this issue: and that within her character there is the working out of the same opposition observed above: while the individual is at odds with her society, she enacts within herself that same conflict. In this case, the Princesse's model for the interpretation of the marriage contract is derived from the influence of history (the ethical challenge set forth by her mother; the influence of her husband and his historical *récit* — the husband who, for the heroine, is largely either absent or past; the heroine's memory; etc.), yet there is a tension with the present, most graphically reflected in the opposition between the absent/past husband and the frequently present Nemours. The model of the past calls for the upholding of obligation, where the attraction of the present would be the striking of a new contract (between the heroine and Nemours) to supersede the old.

Furthermore, as the novel progresses, the protagonist's marriage contract itself takes on for her the aura of history. Even while it is still binding, the contract becomes aligned with history, both as the latter is regarded by the Princesse and as it functions elsewhere in the text: it is the voice of the past which seeks to determine the future. As history thus becomes the decisive factor in the heroine's conflicts noted above, we witness the resolution of those conflicts in the text's conclusion.

Finally, the contract is shown to be the actualization of history. After the crisis of definition, it becomes the "document," unchanging and intransigent, which bears upon the comportment of the individual as well as the individual's relationship with society. Conflict within the contract system is but another manifestation of the tension between the present and the models of the past.

We have arrived at the point where, having isolated two fundamental and parallel binary oppositions in the scheme of action, we may set out the familiar four-part homology of Lévi-Strauss's *Mythologiques* for the sake of validating our impressions and further analyzing the oppositions.[11] On the one hand, we have noted the effects of the chronological tension between the present of action and the past (history) in competition as interpretive models for the heroine to use. Likewise, we have noted that these paradigmatic classes can concurrently be categorized, the first by the occurrence of fortuitous events, and the second, contrarily, by the use of reason. Our findings to this point lead us to postulate these as one set of opposing paradigms of action.

---

[11] See Claude Lévi-Strauss, *Structural Anthropology*, trans. Claire Jacobson and Brooke Grundfest Schoepf (New York and London: Basic Books, 1963), pp. 213 ff.

Catalysts of Action: Social Dynamics   89

On the other hand, we have seen that the individual is systematically set in opposition to the society and that, along these lines, the withdrawal into self is opposed by the outer forces which exercise constraint upon the individual. By extension, we may add respectively to this other set of paradigms the characteristics of the attempt at self-determination, versus the loss or abdication of self-determination through the workings of external pressures.

With these paradigmatic headings as our point of departure, there remains for us to see if the categories and oppositions which they display are sufficiently inclusive to encompass the novel's action reasonably. Admittedly, the use of the procedure as a heuristic device is vulnerable to the criticisms often leveled at Lévi-Strauss, namely that some tacit, evaluative selection process is at work in the construction of paradigms; it is hoped that the results of the effort will outweigh such concerns.

PRESENT	PAST	SELF-DETERMINATION	DETERMINATION IMPOSED
I	II	III	IV
	narrator's historical setting; mother's education		
Princesse meets Clèves at jeweler		attempts to find suitable marriage	
	Reine Dauphine's *récit*		death of Nevers; Princesse marries
Princesse meets Nemours	mother's *récit*; mother's warning		mother's death
		Princesse retreats to country	
	husband's *récit*	Princesse stays in her room	
King's story about astrologer	Reine Dauphine's *récit*		
Nemours steals portrait; is injured on horse	the lost letter episode; Vidame's *récit*	Princesse goes to the country	the *aveu*

Nemours over-hears *aveu*			King Henri II dies
the court changes		Princesse goes to the country	
Nemours spies on Princesse from garden; "gentilhomme" spies on Nemours	husband's death-bed lecture		Clèves dies
		Princesse grieves in seclusion	
	final meeting of Princesse and Nemours		
Nemours spies on Princesse; chance crossing in the park		Princesse retires to convent and home	Princesse dies

Figure 1

We may label the conflict between columns I and II as that over *modes of interpretation*. This is evident not only from the discussion which went before (concerning the immediacy of the present versus the historical model of interpretation as narrated to the protagonist), but also from the constituent elements themselves: in the first case, meaningful events are the products of chance association of persons or things, whereas in column II, the present is explained as an extension of the past. The opposition is fundamentally of a semiotic nature, since it is a question of what constitutes meaning. For one part, meaning is generated by juxtaposition: chance meetings, surprising glances, the overhearing of remarks; in semiotic terms, the constitution of meaning: could here be called *metonymy*. Set in opposition to this, however, are cases in which meaning is seen in continuity, that is to say, in the relationship of resemblance between past and present which we may denote as *metaphor*. Signification by contiguity versus signification by similarity: the locus of opposition here is reduced to its most basic and precise, in the scope of the communication system itself.[12]

[12] For an interesting treatment of other aspects of communication in the novel, see Christian Garaud.

The other principal axis of opposition divides two varying *modes of determination*. In this case, it is a question as to whether the role of the individual will be defined by the self or by greater forces outside the self. Column III shows us cases of introspection and withdrawal into self in an attempt to flee circumstances. Column IV, however, exhibits instances where the character is unable to flee either the mounting pressures of the interpersonal situation or the terms of life. Through this opposition, the influence of the individual is asserted in the summoning of inner forces, or else limited by outer forces which can be neither controlled nor understood.

Structures of similarity between the two fundamental binary oppositions are evident. We recognize that the paradigms of *past* (metaphor) and *self-determination* have in common the function of human reason, the effort to impose reason over the events, the effort to pit human understanding against the chaos of the world. The paradigms of *present* (metonymy) and *determination imposed*, however, share the characteristics of the unforeseeable event and the absence of reason as the world declares its own order independent of human understanding. This tension between reason and chaos is left unresolved, perhaps because of the heroine's ambivalence, perhaps because of the narrator's dispassionate nature; but whatever the explanation, the fact that the opposition is not definitively worked out calls for a conclusion on the part of the reader.

The answer lies in the one thing which is common to all four of our paradigms of action, in the one textual component which produces the chaotic situation of the world and, paradoxically, is called on as the tool of reason to make order out of chaos. This component is history, and we can appreciate now the complexity and stratification of the role it plays in the novel. We began this chapter with the assertion that society and history are mutually dependent for their existence, and we may ask at this point: does humanity shape history or does history shape humanity? The accurate depiction of history in the novel requires an affirmative answer to each part of the question, and the two possibilities are not exclusive of one another due to the dual nature of this pervasive force.

In simplest terms, history is at once both object and subject. It is an object of interpretation and contemplation for characters, it is a token of exchange in conversation, it is edited and shaped by primary and secondary narrators. However, it is also a subject of action, a proleptic force which rises inexorably from the past, the shaper of the future and of human destiny. As a model of intelligibility, it is there for humans to understand and use as a science. As the pattern of existence, on the other hand, history is fate, and as such it is beyond the ken of human understanding or control.

There is a concrete opposition in textual terms, nevertheless, between the two facets of history, and it goes to the heart of the enigmatic quality of the novel's action: in terms of what we have named the *modes of interpretation*, the past's model of resemblance cannot explain away the impact of the present's random associations, any more than Mme de Chartres can, for all her lecturing, prevent her daughter from falling in love. Conversely, the present's metonymic model is blind to historical necessity, to the same extent that Nemours cannot, for all his argumentation, erase the past from the heroine's mind.

History thus dons the mask of Janus. On one side, an idealistic view of the past gives rise to a model for progress in knowledge. On the other side, history is portrayed in pessimistic fashion, endeavoring to show the human mind inferior to the forces of the world. Reinforced are our suspicions that the idealism/pessimism opposition marks the phenomenon of history in all its forms, however it appears in the text: here, as history figures in the structuring of action, idealism and pessimism create the tension of its inner dynamism. The reader's sense of enigma upon completion of the novel may be ascribed to the fact that this tension goes without resolution.

5. *Characterization and Absence*

I

On two levels of the text's composition, we have observed parallel oppositions. First, in the perspective of the narrator there is a clash between the ideal which history holds out for the times in which the action unfolds, and the failure of the characters to live up to that ideal in its entirety. Consequently, we have detected as the result of this opposition an implicit narratorial pessimism, perceptible in the tacit comparison between the perfections of the past and the shortcomings of the present. Second, on the level of the society which the text constructs, the disappointed ideal has to do with love, an idealized love which is frustrated by the realities of social contracts and by the circumstances inherited from history. The result here, as before, is an unspoken kind of pessimism, the portrayal of love as an unattainable good, much sought after, but impossible in view of the inhibiting factors which necessarily surround it.

For the individual in this society, as concerns the level of characterization (or character attribute), the same pessimistic structure is borne out. For characters other than the heroine, there proves to be no favorable environment for their inclinations of love, as for any of a host of reasons, love becomes a disappointed ideal. The king is too jealous, the Vidame de Chartres too inconstant, the queen perhaps too circumspect. Nemours finds his love frustrated by the choice of another person on whom his future depends, while M. de Clèves is thwarted simply by the natural order. With the exception of Clèves, all of these characters encounter opposition for their love in the institution of marriage. The fulfillment of love, however fleeting or unstable, would involve for them the violation of the bonds of marriage. Clèves, on the other hand, gives witness to the rather unencouraging fact that, in the text's world, happiness in love is not fostered by the marriage relationship.

For the heroine, of course, the outlook is no more promising. The ideal of the "call to distinction" comes into conflict with the passions, providing the novel with its central thematic axis of opposition. Duty and passion cannot be reconciled as one is constant while the other is appetitive, one is metaphysical and the other terrestrial, one absolute and the other contingent. These points, which are left unspoken through most of the novel, find expression in the words of the heroine during her last conversation with Nemours (pp. 1242-49). All the while professing deep love for Nemours, the Princesse casts aside all hope for success in love because of no mere technicality, but rather because of the nature of mankind and the nature of love itself. Her abiding assertion is that love is only an appetite, albeit a compelling one. Such attitudes trace a remarkable bond between pastoral literature's Platonic skepticism regarding the passions, on the one hand, and a more general Jansenistic pessimism very much in vogue in the latter part of the seventeenth century, on the other.[1]

At any rate, pessimism on the level of the characterization scheme is perhaps most evident and inherent in the fatalism through which the heroine's choices are compelled. In stating that the ideal is clouded by pessimism at all levels, and that love serves as one facet of the general ideal, we hold that love is an idealized phenomenon in the novel. We may add the nuance that love is *merely* idealized for the heroine, a psychological function that is not brought to fullness. The actualization of love only poses moral problems for her and troubles her *repos*, and so she recognizes the exchange of love with another to be unsettling and problematic at best. Consequently, the only visible signs of love which she exhibits are accidental: until she finally (explicitly) admits her love to Nemours in their last conversation, her only tokens of love are uncontrolled facial expressions, complicity in theft of the portrait, and words and scenes received only accidentally by the object of love. Anxiety is the only feeling which she derives from direct contact with Nemours; it is only in solitude that she feels any degree of happiness with her amorous inclinations (with the sole exception of the letter-writing episode, p. 1189). The same is true

---

[1] See Alain Niderst, *'La Princesse de Clèves' de Mme de Lafayette*, pp. 154-61 for a treatment of the Jansenist sources of the novel's ethical system.

for Nemours who withdraws to contemplate the portrait after stealing it, and who, after spying on the Princesse from the garden at Colomiers, retreats into the forest "pour n'estre vu ni entendu de personne" where "il s'abandonna aux transports de son amour" (p. 1229). Love is paradoxically a phenomenon of solitude and introspection, and the paradox is rooted in the confrontation of pessimism and the ideal.

For the heroine, then, enjoyment is a mental reaction to what remains for her an experience on the ideal plane. In the end she renounces this idealized love, and she does so for philosophical (rather than practical) reasons, choosing in effect to deal with the issue of idealized love in the arena of ideas. Her reasons, which we have cited elsewhere, have nothing to do with Nemours's arguments of satisfied *bienséances*, but rather with metaphysical concerns which pose for her an insurmountable barrier to fulfillment in love.

Defined in terms of heroic characterization and in terms of the individual, the novel is the narrative of the heroine's effort (doomed nonetheless from the start by fate and by preordained circumstances) to reconcile the disparities between the real and the ideal, between duty and love, in her search for happiness and harmony. The reader's interest in the heroic character is tantamount to interest in this quest, since virtually all personal information which is recorded concerning the heroine is pertinent to her moral dilemma. The quest fails, leaving little but pessimistic inferences to be drawn from the narrative as we read it. And all roads lead us to recognize as the most evident technique of characterization the delineation of the heroic figure by a standard, not of physical attribute (for of this we know only that the Princesse is blonde and very beautiful), but of abstract qualities: she is depicted according to how she reasons rather than how she looks, leaving her textual identity in the realm of abstraction, distant in most ways from the world of the reader, to the same extent that she is often absent from the world of the court.

As that effort of reconciliation on the heroine's part fails, she is led to renounce the "real" world and to withdraw to another world, obscure like the one from which she emerges at the beginning of the novel.[2] This other world at novel's end is something of an ideal situation, "non-real" by the standards of society and the court, a combination of convent and private retreat. The life of retreat, austerity, celibacy,

[2] Her first appearance is indeed narrated as something of a surprise event at the court (p. 1113).

and "exemples de vertu inimitables" is carried out in this split setting, giving the reader to wonder why it is so divided, for lack of a detailed or cogent explanation. It would seem that, in some small measure, the effort to reconcile the ideal and the real still goes on after the heroine's withdrawal from society, based solely on the spatial disposition of her action. For it would be consistent with her perennially ambivalent nature that she exercise part of her retreat in private residence (as opposed to convent); and this spatial ambiguity finds a correlative in the narrator's accompanying remarks, where he states that "Mme de Clèves vescut d'une sorte qui ne laissa pas d'apparence qu'elle pust jamais revenir" (p. 1254): only appearances are spoken for, in the same way that it is appearances which are immediately evident to society, but what of the character's real, inner disposition?

Of course, the term "reality" must be understood in the context of fictional discourse. There is no reality for a fairy-tale princess, but the fact that she remains the only imaginary character in an otherwise pseudo-historical narrative underscores both her fictionality and her customary affinity for the ideal to the exclusion of the "real." If indeed there are pessimistic overtones in the novel, they also pertain to the application of intratextual standards to the extratextual world, and vice-versa. The real and the ideal are incompatible, both within the text and in the text's view of itself in the reader's hands.

II

As we observe the attributive process by which the narrator depicts the character of the protagonist, we notice that the technique is one that habitually sets her apart from the rest of her social milieu. Far from sparing in the use of grammatical and logical superlatives to distinguish her, the narrator is effusive from the very moment when the Princesse is introduced. The first substantive which is used to denote the heroine is "une beauté" (p. 1113), and the narrator goes on to set her above her peers on the basis of that characteristic: "...et l'on doit croire que c'étoit une beauté parfaite, puisqu'elle donna de l'admiration dans un lieu où l'on estoit si accoutumé à voir de belles personnes" (p. 1113). The pattern is established whereby the character stands apart from the society which surrounds her. From one point of view, it may be said that the Princesse transcends her society, rising above it to a plane of higher value or merit, incorporating to a singular degree all that can be recognized as good in the world. From quite another point of view, however, it may be noted that the very same characteristics which effect this social distinction also alienate the protagonist from her society, making her a stranger in the midst of her peers.

Characteristics such as beauty, wholly positive and meritorious as they may be, can have this double effect in the novel. In the heroine's case, the simplest explanation for this fact is that, since she is endowed with such superior traits of character, the expectations of narrator, reader and other characters are higher for her than for the rest of society; hence she is set apart from her society (in the view of all concerned) not only in quality, but also in potential. But the same could be said in theory for Nemours who is always described by the narrator as the male counterpart of the heroine in perfection.[3] Thus it would seem necessary to look elsewhere in order to understand the degree of alienation which prevents the Princesse from being completely assimilated into her society.

We must bear in mind all along that the alienation of which we speak is a psychological and largely unilateral phenomenon. At all points the heroine is welcomed into the social circle and never ostracized from it. If she chooses to sequester herself inside or outside that circle, it is by her own decision and out of motivation of which she alone is aware. Her estrangement from society is a result, then, of the other laudable trait which she alone, among the women of her society, exhibits: a keen ethical sense. This leaves her with a rather paradoxical relationship to her society. On the one hand, she attempts genuinely to integrate herself and to play an active social role; she is concerned with goings-on at court and with social appearances; even when she is away from court, she is interested to hear of the social setting which has become her environment. This shows her to be a part of the social unit. Yet on the other hand, she sees clearly all along how her moral system is a poor fit in this world. The point is that there exists a tension for the character as she attempts to arrive at an understanding of her social role. She is at once a popular and vital member of the society in which she sees herself as some kind of misfit.

The indications are manifold that she is the outsider within the court society. At her introduction into the narrative, she arrives as a stranger at the court, provoking an immediate stir with her uncommon beauty. As an ingenue, she shows a need of education in the ways of the

[3] Contrast this, however, with Mme de Chartres's less flattering opinion of Nemours (e.g. p. 1138).

world which are completely strange to her. Subsequently she is often unable in her refined and codified society to play the game of appearances. No fewer than sixteen times throughout the novel is it stated in situations of surprise or crisis that she cannot control her facial expression. At one point, Mme la Dauphine informs her bluntly that her course of action is one that no other woman would have chosen: "...et il n'y a que vous de femme au monde qui fasse confidence à son mary de toutes les choses qu'elle sçait" (p. 1188). In word, if not always in deed, she values sincerity in a society where insincerity is dominant. Certainly her faithfulness to her marriage contract is most atypical for a woman in her situation. And just as certainly, the words of Mme la Dauphine prove to be prophetic indeed as concerns the scene of the *aveu* which has always been viewed as a most extraordinary development by any standard. For the sake of her *repos*, she attempts to extricate herself from society, first at Colomiers, then definitively in retreat. The reader is aware throughout of her constant, vague malaise in society, if only through her habitual state of "agitation" and her expressions of worry over appearances. And finally, on a textual level, we recall that she is (with the exception of her mother, who is functionally a kind of alter ego for her) the only principal character who did not live in reality.

The curious relationship between the protagonist and her society renders it difficult to arrive at a concise explanation of her role in that society. The social unit forms a circle which closes around the heroine, yet which itself does not include her to the extent that she considers herself apart; we the readers may view things in this fashion as well, since most of the narration is fixed in her point of view. It is thus that her rapport with society is problematic because she is at the same time a part of society and apart from it. Understood in light of the nature of the novel's action and its thematic scheme, characterization does observe the pattern of a circle at the center of which we see the protagonist, a fixed point as our vision finds her, a point around which the other characters — the rest of society — revolve in the novel, but a point which is very much apart from many of the goings-on around it. Consequently, the plan of character organization isolates the heroine and causes her to stand out all the more in the reader's eye, "alienating" her and distinguishing her from the rest of her social milieu. And hence, in some measure, that which William O. Goode refers to as the "call to distinction" is also a call to alienation.

III

There is in the novel a kind of progressive focalization process whereby the reader is introduced first, not to the heroine herself, but to her society. Only after the presentation of the global portrait is the reader's attention narrowed to an individual. Since it is the social unit which is carefully and clearly defined prior to the introduction of the protagonist, it is as though the latter is to be viewed not as an individual, but as a member of society. Certainly her actions are best understood when set in relation with the social milieu, even when the relation is one of total contrast with respect to priorities. For the times when she is under society's scrutiny, the reader is looking over society's shoulder. Even when the point of view is fixed in the Princesse, so many of her values are set according to social concerns that she still appears to the reader as focused through the lens of society.

The strange and perhaps most interesting thing about the characterization of the Princesse is her paradoxical and crucial rapport with her social surroundings. Not only does this relationship provide further definition of her moral code (where duty is absolute, while love is increasingly defined as appetitive and relative), but it also paints the background from which she necessarily will stand out. The traits are few which this alienated heroine shares with the rest of the characters who populate the novel. First there is what we may call her human side, that is to say, characteristics which her absolute moral code would brand as frailties: an initial willingness to effect a compromise, jealousy in love, sensitivity to passion, etc. Then, she is, like everyone else, unhappy — an unsurprising development predestined by the history of a society where marriage is predicated on social needs and not on love, where the intercalated narratives concerning women are tales of woe and unfortunate love affairs, where even the king suffers from jealousy to the point of unhappiness. Yet it is difficult to achieve clear perspective on the exact nature of the Princesse's alienation, for while the critics have pointed to the familiar Cornelian thematic of *amour* versus *devoir*, it must be said that duty here is not responsibility to an abstract ideal, as is the case in Corneille. Duty is contractual (i.e. social) in nature, and at any rate, the ideal is not particularly functional in a novel that incorporates latent pessimism to the extent where it is systematic. This is at the heart of the social paradox in characterization.

Depiction of action deflates the ideal which is heralded with respect to the society, by setting up the heroine as counterpoint to the group. Characterization follows the same avenue to devalue the idealized presentation of the individual, thus working out the structure of parallel or reflected oppositions which we first detected in the narrative structure of the novel: there the ostensible idealism of the narrator's vision is undermined by the doubt which his historicism provokes; as concerns society, perfection and *éclat* prove to be but a veneer; in the accumulation of signs of the individual character, the opposition is again borne out. While we are told, sometimes by the heroine herself, that she is good and without blame, the fact remains that perfection is an unattainable goal. For if, as during the scene of the *aveu*, she swears that she has shown no sign of yielding in the face of temptation, she admits to herself (e.g. p. 1172) having shown marks of her illicit love. The systematic and parallel tension at all levels between the ideal and its failure, creates a highly significant structure that brings to light a cogent ironic reading of the novel.

IV

An important component in character construction is the individual's appreciation and understanding of the written word, and the relationship between that individual and what may be called the institution of writing. It is interesting to note that, while no other literary work is mentioned by name,[4] and while no character is ever shown in the act of reading a book, individuals and the society retain a rather high degree of literacy because of the practice of letter-writing, the most suitable vehicle for communication in *absence*. The letter is the concrete token of exchange, the product of the circumspect process of encoding the emotions in the form of the written word, yet also the product of a betrayal since the vividness of emotion is attenuated through its translation into stylized language. The restrained tenor of the written word is thus a mask for emotion, as letters tend to be written in moments of crisis and to serve as a means of urgent communication, failing the presence of the addressee. When characters pore over them, as the Princesse does with the letter of the Vidame,

---

[4] Marie Stuart does make passing reference to the Princess having read the "contes" of Marguerite, that is, the *Heptameron* (p. 1162). John D. Lyons views this allusion as the text's means of associating itself with the *novella* tradition; see Lyons, p. 385, note 5. In his article, Lyons goes on to study the generic modes of discourse in the novel and the implications of narrative modes of discourse.

letters take the place of books as objects of study. By the same token, given the response which the written word elicits, writing is set on the same affective plane with other visual objects, thus serving not only as semantic systems, but also as tangible metonymic tokens which bring the absent party closer to presence. Still, the nature of language and the absence inherent in the system of writing pose problems of clarity which do not beset the rest of visual communication: writing's indirectness and the absence of the writer can cause confusion for the one who reads.

Reading affords parameters according to which the composition of characters may be defined. In the particular case of the heroine, whose habits and aptitudes are more clearly delineated than those of others in the text, reading is a helpful sign for the categorizing of characterization. Because of her inability to reconstruct the letter belonging to the Vidame (p. 1189), despite the fact that she had spent the entire previous evening reading and re-reading it carefully, she would have to be classified as something of a poor reader. Her lack of deftness in reading is all the more evident when one contrasts it with her function as narratee: she remembers scrupulously that which is told to her as a story of the past, but her ability to grasp the essence of what she reads is far less pronounced.

With the objectification of the linguistic system, there appears to materialize some kind of barrier to communication. In short, the written word is less effective than the spoken word. The former is error-prone, subject to prolonged, distorting scrutiny and re-interpretation. The spoken word, however, is less palpable and thus more direct, more transparent, and efficient outside the realm of love in which it wields little power. This translates directly into contrasting effectiveness: where in one case her memory of the written word proves so ineffective that she is unable to reconstruct a letter which touched her profoundly, she appears nevertheless able to recall in detail the historical narratives that are addressed to her.

As narratee of the oral accounts of history, the heroine appears to be much more attentive and sensitive to nuances of meaning. In good part, her role is similar to that of the reader, with the notable exception that the latter is ostensibly encountering information in the written form, while *she* is understood to be hearing it. Both do share the role of student of history. For the reader, it is the scheme of events, fictional or otherwise, which are taken from the past and set down in language fraught with ambiguities and unresolved oppositions; in the case of the heroine, the communication of history proves to be markedly less problematic, possibly because the absence of past characters and events is vividly compensated for in her mind by secondary narrators who become voices of conscience. For the Princesse, the problem is not remotely one of reliability or detail in her understanding of narratives to which she listens, but rather it is her interpretation of this kind of history and her reaction to it which are capital.

This points up a structural opposition between the active and the passive, wherein history calls on the character to study history and to accept its fixed model, while society and the world beckon to the character to define for herself what it is that she will become. If she accepts the preordained model of history, she sacrifices self-determination and is constrained to abide by an inherited moral code. If, on the other hand, she chooses the active role of self-determination, she sacrifices the tenets of conscience and betrays many expectations. As a thematic opposition, this confrontation of destiny and free will is not in the least unfamiliar for the latter part of the seventeenth century. But as a structural component in this novel, it translates into the spatial division of the heroine's life between presence at court and absence in solitude, the latter of which wins out in the end.

That history is absolute and a source of uncompromising moral direction for the Princesse comes as no surprise at this juncture in our work. But her understanding of those narrators who recount history to her, and her personal attitude toward them, are also significant. The fact is that, after the deaths of her mother and husband, those characters become absolute in the mind of the Princesse, counter to the relativity of passion, and they function as kinds of deities for her in the absence of God and religion. Concern for social appearances, and a code which sets out only to surpass social codes, are what constitute the worldly moral system of the heroine, but it is no less absolute (at least in principle) than the most rigorous moral code in Racine.

It is paradoxical, then, that the side of the passive model—that of the strict moral code—has at least the activity of spoken language (narration) working for it, while the seemingly more dynamic side of relativity deals in symbolic, figurative communication, either through the non-verbal means of expression or through a static form of representation (portraits, paintings, material possessions of the beloved, such as the "canne des Indes" and the scarf). It is interesting to note that the heroine keeps no such memorabilia or portrait of her mother or husband; these two remain as a psychological and historical influence, defining the disposition of the heroine's terrestrial life. Her love is more graphic and tangible, paradoxically immediate since it is perceptible to the senses, but only in the absence of the beloved person. It is thus that history is portrayed as the ideal, while love becomes idealized after passing through the senses. The debate between the two is set on an equal footing at the level of the ideal, but sign systems remain distinct and compartmentalized. History communicates through processes of introspection and memory in order to bring its moral code to the fore; love is pursued along avenues of sensory communication other than that of the direct linguistic. Hence the facet of character in the novel which relates to love both communicates and is communicated in such sensory terms. The heroine's blushes and facial reactions are visible to Nemours as well as to the reader. The night scene in the garden "cabinet" is described in very sensual terms (pp. 1227 ff.), and Nemours, for his part throughout the novel, relies on the visual to collect and to transmit signs of love.

V

To what extent, then, is it that the reader is to be seen as mirrored in the character of the protagonist (as narratee)? If we attempt, for example, to form a composite semiology of the narratee or implied reader, certainly we are drawn to the role of the heroine as narratee, for in this role she is most active and most effective. On the one hand, there is an obvious similarity of function between the narratee-character and the narratee on the overall textual level. To some degree, the implied reader (or the *reader*, for that matter) is portrayed thematically in the Princesse, gathering and analyzing information concerning events which are understood in one way or another to be historical. By the same token, however, when we elevate the question to the textual level, that is to say, when we as readers of a novel take a view of the novel's protagonist as an aesthetic entity, there is raised necessarily and automatically some kind of barrier that separates the observer from the observed, a distance in which the dynamic of absence comes into play. In the case of *La Princesse de Clèves*, the absence which circumscribes the heroine is made all the more acute by the thematic scheme, the social structure, and the characterization technique of the novel: character is sequestered from God, perhaps as a function of scriptorial choice; she is a stranger in the social crowd, alienated, as we have seen, by compelling moral priorities, separated from the world by a disparity of world view. And if this process of alienation were to endear the protagonist to the reader—tempt the reader to identify with her, in the true sense of the phrase—by virtue of the character's abstraction from her own world and time and from the shortcomings of the human condition, there are still signs which render her absent from the reader, set apart by what we may view as a system of metatextual alienation. Here we refer to signs which reflect the literary process and even mimic representationally the activity of the reader, but which serve to differentiate or distance the reader from his textual counterpart precisely in keeping with the aesthetic ontology of the latter. In other words, despite any affinity of function or interest with the character, the reader is compelled to recognize the degree to which that character is aesthetically objectified within the world of the novel, and hence absent from the world where the act of reading takes place.

If not to remind the reader of this quality of apartness in the character, why would the narrator end his account with the word "inimitables?" Why would a totally fictional character be introduced into a pseudo-historical narrative? Why else would history produce in her an anachronistic set of values which in effect predestines her retreat from society? Why is this seclusion divided spatially between the "maison religieuse" and the heroine's own home, to the same extent that the opposition which separates her from her society is a divisive force within her own mind? Finally, even if these and other paradoxes in the novel were afforded a tidy and logical conclusion, how could one reconcile the opposition of almost generic proportion whereby a fairy-tale princess appears in a fairy-tale world only to encounter a disappointment of the ideal and an impossibility of human happiness?

We would propose to answer all of these questions by defining the textual technique of characterization by the dynamic of distance. The technique is one of tracing or implying a metaphysical distance between reader and character, not merely for the sake of underscoring the character's fictionality (although this is accomplished), but also to render the character difficult to understand, difficult to define either in terms of the reader's world or by the standards of the fictive world in which she supposedly lives. She is, in this sense, absent from both worlds. We have already likened her to the center point around which the social circle closes, but which the circle itself does not include. This is perhaps the most graphic and accurate model for the novel's heroic characterization. But she is also difficult to visualize both for this sort of "strangeness" or apartness, and for lack of detail in narrative description. Ultimately the reader must settle for historical retrospect on a character who acts by a criterion of distinction, and through whose eyes we see only how different she seeks to be. By this technique, the text's magic is worked through the fictive illusion created as it might be with any other novel, and despite the mirage before our eyes, this heroine remains impossible to rationalize or categorize. Present in fiction, she may still be absent from the reader's understanding, set apart by a measuring stick of logic because of her inconsistency, finally absent (literally and figuratively) from her society for all of the characteristics that alienate her. Thus it is fitting, if paradox is to beget consistency, that the heroine disappear at the end of the novel into the absence and obscurity from which she emerged at the beginning.

VI

If we visualize the Princesse as situated in the center of the social circle, we readily imagine that she is under scrutiny, standing apart from the rest of humanity, equidistant from every point on the circle. Such is the case at the social level. Elevated to the textual level, the question of the "heroine apart" calls our attention to the dual nature of the opposition between central point of focus and the social perimeter around it, especially as pertains to perception in narration. Since the locus of narrative point of view furnishes the reader's perspective, much important information concerning the society comes to the reader through the impressions of the protagonist. Thus, one way to assess the text's plan of charactarization—the development of characters and their relative effectiveness—is to see the heroine, for narrative purposes, as the hub of the social circle and the unifying point of presentation. How she relates to the rest of characters then determines *their* roles and effectiveness.

The thematic of distance or absence/presence provides important parameters for the sketching out of central character relationships. With the opposing emotional forces personified in M. de Clèves and Nemours respectively, it is a question of the differing ways in which the Princesse recalls them to immediacy in her mind during their absence. For her husband, the process is a historical (necessarily linguistic) one of memory when it is not one of actual duty, itself a historical phenomenon. This is a natural consequence of the fact that

M. de Clèves is a man of words, basing his claims on the lessons of the past (historical *récit*) and the contracts of the past. And thus it is his words which render him present to his wife in a given moment of crisis: e.g. "Ce que M. de Clèves luy avoit dit sur la sincérité... luy revint dans l'esprit" (p. 1166); otherwise, it is the memory of her duty to him that lends force to his side of the struggle in the heroine's mind. Such means are called for as, in the main, M. de Clèves is a character of absence—often absent from where the heroine is, discreet and usually self-effacing. Where the Princesse is concerned, he is as distant from her spatially as he is from her affections.

Contrarily, Nemours is a character of presence, and his relationship with the heroine depends on physical proximity to her: when they first meet, they dance together; throughout the novel, he is compelled to seek her presence as he invents pretexts time after time to be near her; the heroine herself even recognizes this physical nature of their relationship, as it is narrated:

> Elle ne pouvoit s'empescher d'estre troublée de sa veue, et d'avoir pourtant du plaisir à le voir; mais quand elle ne le voyoit plus et qu'elle pensoit que ce charme qu'elle trouvoit dans sa vue estoit le commencement des passions, il s'en falloit peu qu'elle ne crût le haïr par la douleur que luy donnoit cette pensée. (p. 1141)

For Nemours himself, when he is deprived of the physical presence of his beloved at the end of the novel, his love loses its ardor and dies.

It is in Nemours's relativity to the whereabouts of the heroine that this issue of presence is most striking. While the husband is responding to obligations which call him away, Nemours finds ways to sidestep such obligations in order to be near her. At several points when M. de Clèves is at court, Nemours attempts to visit the Princesse at her *maison de campagne*. During the scene of the recreating of the Vidame's letter (p. 1189), the heroine is supposedly reassured by the "presence" of her husband who, nevertheless, is not in the room nor anywhere to be seen after the goings and comings surrounding the incident; prior to this scene, it is M. de Clèves who brings Nemours to his wife's room and immediately departs "...chez le Roy, qui venoit de l'envoyer quérir. M. de Nemours demeura seul auprès de Mme de Clèves, comme il le pouvoit souhaiter" (p. 1184).

Clearly there is a spatial opposition of presence between the two rivals who, for the most part, are mutually exclusive in this respect: when one is with her, the other tends not to be there; quite often, it is M. de Clèves who is absent. After he dies, Nemours continues to be the character of presence, and his presence is not one of words (like that of M. de Clèves). Rather, it is one of sight and silence. For, as the narrator makes clear,

> Les paroles les plus obscures d'un homme qui plaist donnent plus d'agitation que des déclarations ouvertes d'un homme qui ne plaist pas. (p. 1157)

From the merchant's window (pp. 1238-39) and in the park (pp. 1239-40), no words are spoken by Nemours, but his presence is acutely sensed by the heroine. As has been the case throughout the novel, Nemours is the observer whose presence, rather than his words, influences the Princesse. He knows (and relies on) what he is able to accomplish with his personal presence: maintaining high visibility in society, complaining when his amorous endeavors are deprived of direct contact (e.g. p. 1241), etc. In this he is quite the opposite of M. de Clèves whose presence is anything but formidable, but who maintains no less a great influence of memory in his absence.

The Princesse may chide her husband for his absence:

> Je vous attendis tout hier,... et je vous dois faire des reproches de n'estre pas venu comme vous me l'aviez promis. (p. 1143)

But it is not his physical presence which counts for him. Instead, his is a psychological force with the full power of history behind it, and Nemours himself is the one who most vividly recognizes this fact when he incredulously asks of the heroine during their last encounter: "Ah! madame,... quel fantôme de devoir opposez-vous à mon bonheur?" (p. 1245). M. de Clèves indeed plays the role of *fantôme*, even before his death, for he is at once the heroine's voice of conscience as well as the point of characterization where the currents of *histoire* and *devoir* converge.

So, it is fitting that the device which activates the Princesse's mind with regard to her husband (and all he stands for) be the memory of words—*his* medium of communication. At a moment of crisis, it is recollection which charts the course of duty for her:

> Elle se souvenoit de tout ce que Mme de Chartres luy avoit dit en mourant et des conseils qu'elle luy avoit donnez de prendre toutes sortes de partis, quelques difficiles qu'ils pussent estre, plutost que de s'embarquer dans une galanterie. Ce que M. de Clèves luy avoit dit sur la sincérité, en parlant de Mme de Tournon, luy revint dans l'esprit; (p. 1166).

For Nemours, on the other hand, the means which summon him to immediacy in the protagonist's thoughts are not verbal or historical. Rather, they are the visual stimuli, like the painting of his likeness which she procures, and (as our structural schema in the preceding chapter might lead us to expect) the object which she associates metonymically with Nemours, like the "canne des Indes."

It is an evident conclusion, given all the constraints that we have noted as influencing the Princesse, that she chooses for herself according to the model of absence. As the novel moves toward sealing the destinies of its characters, she will necessarily withdraw from a society which she cannot change and which itself is unable to integrate her fully. She is cast in the center of a social circle, two of whose members set contrasting models of behavior (or even existence) before her. Nemours and M. de Clèves stand in that circle, their attention focused on the heroine, and poised in direct thematic opposition with one another. In light of the text's narrative structure (the locus of most of the narrative's point of view, the nature of the protagonist's stature in the narrator's eyes, etc.), the brunt of the opposition will bear psychologically upon the Princesse; likewise, the involvement of the other principals is effected separately, in absentia, and for an understandable reason: a direct and personal confrontation between Clèves and Nemours (which never does transpire in the novel) would take choice and responsibility away from the heroine, reducing her to the role of the "object fought for," the object of another's quest. In other words, she would be rendered the observer, while the focus of narrative attention would shift to the male rivalry. But as it is, the thematic opposition which stands behind this rivalry is worked out, not in contact, but through the medium which remains the focal point of narrative and the narrative center of the text's social circle—the Princesse herself—in the absence of both husband and Nemours.

For the rivals, Clèves is aloof and pensive, and Nemours is active, attentive, and impetuous. While Clèves is absent, Nemours endeavors to make his presence felt. If Clèves is insecure, Nemours is daring and self-confident. Clèves, on the one hand, is not recorded as participating in any of the athletic events narrated; Nemours, for his part, excels in all of them, attesting to his vitality in the physical domain. And finally, the historical affinities discussed above set the two characters in mutual opposition as they vie for the heroine's affections, much in the favor of Nemours. Yet, despite an obvious inferiority of resources, Clèves maintains parity for his command of the extrapersonal weapon—the moral code, or contract system, which rises up out of history to prevail upon the heroine's judgment.

Among the qualities of characterization that the text recognizes as praiseworthy, certain oppositions remain forever unresolved. Which of the two male principals has the narrator's approbation and the reader's sympathy? Is it Clèves who stands as an obstacle to love and happiness in his role of moral guardian? Or could it be the "perfect" Nemours who, nonetheless, stands justly accused of undesirable traits, not the least of which is that of the inconstant lover at the end? If Clèves is heroic, he cuts rather a pale figure and has none of the personal characteristics that command admiration. But if Nemours completely embodies the heroic code, it is impossible to account for his involvement in the death of a supposed friend, or his callous and opportunistic intentions thereabouts. Neither character is wholly deserving or undeserving to be the bearer of the positive standard. But as to which one is in the right, by moral or sentimental standards, the text does not say; obviously it takes great care to leave the opposition in the balance.

The same situation is seen within the characterization of the Princesse. She is not definitively cast as either totally innocent or guilty of complicity, virtuous or coy, austere or coquettish. The text is careful to forego a binding, even prejudicial, assessment of her character. Is her withdrawal from society a positive moral action or a penetential rite? Issues like these can spark lengthy critical debate, but the point is not that the reader should offer interpretation where the text is silent. Rather, it is the very fact that the tensions and ambiguities remain crucial and active well after the reader has closed the book. Instead of heralding the triumph of one side over the other, the narrative scheme is obviously designed to feature the controversy itself. To be sure, both praise and blame of the heroine and other characters are not lacking in the corpus of the novel's critical works. However, in a novel where history compels a quest for worldly morality and then tacitly defeats its own purposes, no great harmonious resolution should be expected or inferred.

The text, then, is a mystery in its moral self-portraiture, and its plan of characterization is a part of that enigma. Any effort to label characters as standing for or against the positive values meets with significant opposition. But these traits cannot be out of place in a novel where characters are unsure of themselves as they strive for predestinately impossible ideals. Nor could such signs be viewed as aimless in a work where optimism and pessimism stand locked throughout in mutual contradiction. If there were a resolution to be found within the text, it would bear capital significance, and it would certainly shape the reader's appreciation of the characterization structure. However, no such resolution is made definite or even implied, therefore the reader must choose: either to extend reading into the domain of surmise and inference, or to reflect the anomaly back onto the structure of the text and thus to make of it a model for the reading of the novel. The latter approach would appear to illuminate better the text as it is written.

Conclusion

One of the possible pitfalls of monographic writing is inherent in the nature of the task at hand. To isolate one aspect of a literary work for study is like focusing one's attention on a single thread in a tapestry: the more significance it is shown to bear, and the more integral a part it is shown to be, that much greater is the temptation to attribute all significance and global artistic essence to it. But if recent aesthetic theory has taught us anything, it is that the notion of meaning in art defies confinement or reduction. It is hoped that this trap has been avoided in our treatment of history in *La Princesse de Clèves*.

To do the topic justice, however, it must be said that history takes on meaning, and generates meaning, on so many levels as to call attention to itself—not as a lone structural axis of concentration, but certainly as a vital one. As a structuring principle it does lend organization and community of purpose to much material on all levels of the text's composition. Thus, while history is not the only medium of structure and significance in the novel, it still merits close study for the fact that all of those levels owe to it something which they contribute to the composite.

It has seemed difficult at every new turn to achieve a secure grasp on the phenomenon of history in this novel. First of all, on the most inclusive level of the text's presentation, we are dealing with a "historical novel"—something of an anomalous rubric since history supposedly aims, by common understanding, to be a factual chronicle, while a novel is generally understood to be fictitious. Yet the two media are melted together with scarcely a qualitative distinction drawn between them, leaving the reader to wonder about the relative effects of historical perspective and content on the work's composition and creation.

Then on another level, that of narrative structure, history (aside from giving a mirror image of the principal narration) forms much of what J.D. Lyons calls the "discourse of wisdom," that component of narration which will be intended to serve in turn thematically, as a model of interpretation for characters in their world.[1] But, as Lyons points out, there is also "...the failure of the courtly discourse of wisdom to contain reality within norms and examples" (Lyons, p. 396) to the satisfaction of the characters' minds; on the one hand, it takes time for either the prescriptive or the metaphorical nature of intercalated history to become apparent to the heroine, and on the other, she finds herself alienated from the common practice of wisdom in the world. The lag between normality and the "discourse of wisdom" Lyons identifies as *paradox*.

Finally, there would remain the question of "l'économie du récit" as the novel participates in the broad conventions of literarity, set against the conclusions reached in monographic study of history in the text. In specific terms, do we run the risk of attributing to the dynamic of history (i.e. the properties of prolepsis and fatality that we deem assigned to it) effects which more properly belong to the conventions of fictive narration? Can one overstate the case of history in the novel? Can one confuse it with the exigencies of *vraisemblance* as Gérard Genette envisions them, operative in any given piece of fictional prose?[2]

This question of motivation is the most fundamental of all, for it challenges the very premise from which this study proceeds. To formulate a reply, we must first clarify the issue, even if it is in retrospect. Never should we lose sight of the fact that *La Princesse* offers a spectrum of possibilities for relating elements of the narrative to the implied reader's understanding. Narrator and characters alike appeal to principles of human psychology, for example, to "justify" actions or to propose plausible motivation; the actual plausibility or *vraisemblance* aside, areas of knowledge (like psychology, politics, or

---

[1] John D. Lyons.
[2] *Figures II* (Paris: Editions du Seuil, 1969), pp. 71-98.

what Jonathan Culler calls "cultural *vraisemblance*"[3]) are referred to explicitly or implicitly in order for the narrative to "seem logical."

History (as the implied reader may be presumed familiar with French national history and court tradition) is another one of these areas of knowledge—one among several, it may be argued. However, the cardinal point is that history, while serving this purpose, is also much more than that. If it were merely an extratextual fund from which background is drawn, this study would justly be accused of making much ado about little. But the novel opens with a detailed passage of history, setting a tenor and context for the rest of the narration, and giving the telling of history an exalted status. Then there is the introduction of historicism into the thematic scheme of the novel (principally by Mme de Chartres and the Reine Dauphine) whereby characters recognize and discuss the bearing of the past upon the understanding of the present, and exhort the young heroine to do the same. There is likewise history's subtle but systematic foreshadowing function. And finally, add to all these qualities the role which the recounting of history plays in the novel's narrative strategy, and there emerges a whole plan of importance which goes far beyond the initial purpose of *vraisemblance*. More than a mere foundation for "logic," a system of intelligence and meaning is animated by history at so many levels in the text as to warrant careful attention and detailed explanation. To provide this explanation, the present study was undertaken.

In light of all the qualities and textual value which history embodies, it is a worthy enterprise to isolate it for close consideration as a multilevel axis, one which governs many elements in the text's organization at the levels mentioned. The function of motivation and *vraisemblance* is exercised at one of these strata, but our key point is that the study of this role does not at all exhaust the topic's resources or integrate it into an inclusive reading of the novel. *Vraisemblance*, thematic motif, narrative technique, structuring device: history indeed appears as the point to which many roads lead as one endeavors to chart the patterns of the novel's organization. And if it is such a

---

[3] See Jonathan Culler on the notion of "cultural *vraisemblance*" in *Structuralist Poetics* (London: Routledge and Kegan Paul, 1975), pp. 141-45. Consider in this light the remarks of Nemours to the Vidame, reproaching the latter for his indiscretion (concerning the Queen): "Elle est Italienne et Reine, et par conséquent pleine de soupçons, de jalousie et d'orgueil;..." (p. 1182).

point of strategic convergence, history's significance has not been overstressed in this study.

At this juncture, one might object that, admitting the importance of history to an even greater degree, it produces inexorably a lapsus between the "discourse of wisdom" and "reality" (all within the fiction, of course); this being the case, a study of history in *La Princesse* cannot proceed beyond the practical paradox identified by J.D. Lyons. The point is precisely that study should not go beyond, but rather should dwell on, this paradox whose opposition gives life to the narrative. The dynamics and broad scope of paradox encompass all of the action which follows its course as though impelled by the opposition between society's past and society's present. But were this not the case, it would even suffice to say that the critic's task is not to find logic *in* the text, but rather to explain the logic (or illogic) *of* the text. In the present case, the study of history goes a long way toward this end.

Having spoken of the intratextual concerns complicating our topic, we may also turn our attention to the relationship between the narrative and the extratextual history that it includes—in other words, the inevitable question as to how much influence is worked upon the composition of the text by reality. We speak now, not of the reality of *vraisemblance*, nor of the fictional network which poses as reality within the confines of the fiction, but of the real world whose history prompts the use of the term "historical novel." It is a complicated issue, one whose discussion bridges the gap between a world of the verifiable and a "world" of the arbitrary. And given the greatly variable nature of such a bridge as one moves from text to text in the corpus of historical novels, discussion tends to remain case-specific instead of generic.

Generalizations that can be made are, first, that extra-textual history serves as some sort of model (for structure, plot, character, etc.), and then that narrative often assumes a teleological quality for its association with the genuinely historical model, at least as concerns events surrounding a fictional plot. Beyond these, the characteristics of history as a textual tool become unique and dynamic, and for *La Princesse* we have attempted to explain this dynamism within the scope of the text itself.

History outside the text has the particular function of establishing a chain of signification for the reader. By this is meant specifically that prolepsis (about which we and others have spoken at length) does not merely remain a property of the level of action. True, characters may make proleptic remarks which bear greater meaning than the literal to the informed reader who knows what they, the characters, do not; this occurs, for example, with Henri II and Marie Stuart. By itself, the phenomenon constitutes a simple case of verbal irony. The reader, however, may then transfer that foreshadowing process to lines of fictive action, triggering a proleptic reflex which has become conditioned in the reader, manipulated not by the narrator (whom we presume unaware of the difference between real historical data and fiction), but by the authorial presence (which directs the narrative voice for effect). Thus, when the reader senses that the principles spoken by Mme de Chartres and M. de Clèves will eventually be put to the test, a structural irony is in place since it is clear (from the "lesson" that *history* teaches us) that scriptor and reader know more than narrator and character know.

And what of the tacit pessimism we have so often detected and associated inextricably with the narrator's overtly idealistic view of history? What conclusive statements can be made for it? Clearly this pessimism is an inherent trait of the novel's historiographic process. For the most part, the historic vision which produces this narrative is a classical one, examining in retrospect, projecting the world view of a historian of the 1670s over the events of the preceding century, i.e. projecting the history of Louis XIV over that of Henri II and François II combined.

So what motivation for pessimism can we infer in this *Weltanschauung* and historiographic technique? We may look to events and developments which transpired in the interim that could conceivably color a historian's view. First, there is the consolidation of power in the monarchy which rendered the nobility ineffectual and thus left untapped the potentials of past perfections. The historian would necessarily view the period of time (described in the narrative) as the nobility's last great moment, destined to end soon under Richelieu and Mazarin. Second, Jansenism (whether espoused or not by the historian/scriptor) succeeded in raising moral standards in general, and it caused the intellectual community to debate the value of phenomena on the earthly plane. At the very least, the notion of attaining the Good on earth was called into question; this *debate* is certainly mirrored in the paradox (left unresolved) of pessimism and idealism in *La Princesse*. Finally, the historiographic vision which is critical of social disorder in the past could very well be projecting its own guilt concerning social disorder in its present time. Here the questions of the mutability of the code of hierarchy, the growing influence of the bourgeoisie, and even the confusion of the Fronde, all come into play. These are profound tensions for which the text offers no solutions. Instead, the novel may be read as setting them before the reader, "disguised," as it were, in the setting of the previous century. So if the historian's idealistic façade is cracked, explanation may certainly be found in the stresses which underlie the writing of history.

To conclude, we have at times drawn near the arena of reader response which would certainly provide the topic for another book. With respect to the present study's limited scope, however, we recognize complexity behind the appearances of straightforwardness, beginning with the intertwining of historical and pseudo-historical presentation. A narrative scheme of this sort makes it a difficult task indeed to abstract the true history from the whole narration for the purpose of studying its effects on a novel of fiction. Nevertheless, the composite text holds forth a rich and intricate plan of presentation that calls for attention by its own merit, in addition to suggesting further work on its vital, organic association of histories, real and imaginary.

To view *La Princesse de Clèves* not merely as a love story, but in a larger perspective as the portrayal of a courtly society's inner workings, is necessarily to pose questions and formulate models of reading that bear upon this complex brand of historiography. It is hoped that these pages have provided some sense of what history and society, those two confluent forces, contribute to the text. Even if questions remain and models continue to call for revision, our reading can proceed from an awareness of the novel's global nature—love story, to be sure, but also the chronicle of life at court.

Bibliography

Text

Lafayette, Madame de. *La Princesse de Clèves*. In *Romanciers du XVIIe Siècle*. Paris: Editions Gallimard, 1958, pp. 1105-1254.

Critical Works Consulted

Adam, Antoine. *Histoire de la littérature française*. Vol. IV. Paris: Editions Domat, 1954.

Alter, Jean V. "C'est moi qui parlons: le jeu des narrateurs dans *Francion*." *French Forum*, 5 (1980), 99-105.

Boorsch, Jean. "Madame de Lafayette and the Manipulation of History." *American Society of Legion of Honor Magazine*, 46 (1975), 97-109.

Brooks, Peter. *The Novel of Worldliness: Crébillon, Marivaux, Laclos, Stendhal*. Princeton: Princeton University Press, 1969.

Dédéyan, Charles. *Mme de Lafayette*. Paris: Société d'Edition de l'Enseignement Supérieur, 1955.

Doubrovsky, Serge. "*La Princesse de Clèves*: une interprétation existentielle." *La Table Ronde*, 138 (June 1959), 36-51.

Fontaine-Bussac, Geneviève. "L'Ethique dans *La Princesse de Clèves*." *Revue d'Histoire Littéraire de la France*, 77 (1977), 500-06.

Fraisse, Simone. "Le 'repos' de Madame de Clèves." *Esprit*, 29 (November 1961), 560-67.

Garaud, Christian. "Le Geste et la parole: remarques sur la communication amoureuse dans *La Princesse de Clèves*." *XVIIe Siècle*, 121 (1978), 257-68.

Goldin, Jeanne. "Maximes et fonctionnement narratif dans *La Princesse de Clèves*." *Papers on Seventeenth Century Literature*, 10, No. 2 (1978), 155-76.

Goode, William O. "A Mother's Goals in *La Princesse de Clèves*: Worldly and Spiritual Distinction." *Neophilologus*, 56 (1973), 398-406.

Gregorio, Laurence A. "Implications of the Love Debate in *L'Astrée*," *French Review*, 56, No. 1 (October 1982), 31-39.

Haig, Stirling. *Madame de Lafayette*. New York: Twayne, 1970.

Kaps, Helen Karen. *Moral Perspective in 'La Princesse de Clèves'*. Eugene, Oregon: University of Oregon Books, 1968.

Kuizenga, Donna. *Narrative Strategies in 'La Princesse de Clèves'*. Lexington, Kentucky: French Forum Publishers, 1976.

Kusch, Manfred. "Narrative Technique and Cognitive Modes in *La Princesse de Clèves*." *Symposium*, 30 (Winter 1976), 308-24.

Lawrence, Francis L. "*La Princesse de Clèves* Reconsidered." *French Review*, 39 (1965-1966), 15-21.

Lyons, John D. "Narrative, Interpretation and Paradox: *La Princesse de Clèves*." *Romanic Review*, 72, No. 4 (November 1981), 383-400.

Malandin, Pierre. "Ecriture de l'histoire dans *La Princesse de Clèves*." *Littérature*, 36 (1979), 19-36.

Moore, Ann M. "History and Temporal Structure in *La Princesse de Clèves*." *Proceedings of the Eighth Annual Meeting of the Western Society for French History*, 8 (1981), 131-46.

⸺⸺⸺. "Temporal Structure and Reader Response in *La Princesse de Clèves*." *French Review*, 56, No. 4 (March 1983), 563-71.

Niderst, Alain. *'La Princesse de Clèves': le roman paradoxal*. Paris: Larousse, 1973.

⸺⸺⸺. *'La Princesse de Clèves' de Madame de Lafayette*. Paris: Nizet, 1977.

Respaut, Michèle. "Un texte qui se dérobe: narrateur, lecteur et personnages dans *La Princesse de Clèves*." *L'Esprit Créateur*, 19, No. 1 (1979), 64-73.

Scott, J. W. "The 'Digressions' of the *Princesse de Clèves*." *French Studies*, 11 (1957), 315-21.

Singerman, Alan J. "History as Metaphor in Mme de Lafayette's *La Princesse de Clèves*." *Modern Language Quarterly*, 36 (1975), 261-71.

Turnell, Martin. *The Novel in France*. London: Hamish Hamilton, 1950.

Vigée, Claude. "*La Princesse de Clèves* et la tradition du refus." *Critique*, 16, No. 159-60 (August-September 1960), 723-54.

Zimmermann, Eléonore M. *La Liberté et le destin dans le théâtre de Jean Racine*. Stanford French and Italian Studies 24. Saratoga, Calif.: Anma Libri, 1982.

Theoretical Texts Consulted

Booth, Wayne C. *Rhetoric of Fiction*. Chicago: University of Chicago, 1961.

Culler, Jonathan. *The Pursuit of Signs: Semiotics, Literature, Deconstruction*. Ithaca: Cornell University Press, 1981.

⸺⸺⸺. *Structuralist Poetics: Structuralism, Linguistics and the Study of Literature*. London: Routledge and Kegan Paul, 1975.

Debray-Genette, Raymonde. "Les Figures du récit dans *Un coeur simple*." *Poétique*, No. 3 (1970), pp. 348-64.

Frye, Northrop. *Anatomy of Criticism: Four Essays*. Princeton: Princeton University Press, 1957.
Genette, Gérard. *Figures II*. Paris: Editions du Seuil, 1969.
Lévi-Strauss, Claude. *Structural Anthropology*, trans. Claire Jacobson and Brooke Grundfest Schoepf. New York and London: Basic Books, 1963.
White, Hayden. *Metahistory*. Baltimore: The Johns Hopkins University Press, 1973.

Period Texts

Racine, Jean. *Andromaque*. Paris: Larousse, 1959.
———. *Bérénice*, in *Oeuvres complètes*. Vol. I. Paris: Gallimard, 1950.
———. *Britannicus*. Paris: Larousse, 1971.
———. *Phèdre*. Paris: Larousse, 1971.